Cities of Mughul India

Delhi Agra and Fatehpur Sikri

Delhi Agra and Fatehpur Sikri

Cities of Mughul India

Gavin Hambly

Photographs Wim Swaan

G. P. Putnam's Sons
New York

To
PERCIVAL SPEAR
Chronicler of Old Delhi
this book
is respectfully dedicated

Fig. 1   Babur entering the Palace of Sultan Ibrahim at Agra.

Designed by Harold Bartram

Library of Congress Catalog Card Number: 68–31214

Printed in Great Britain

Contents

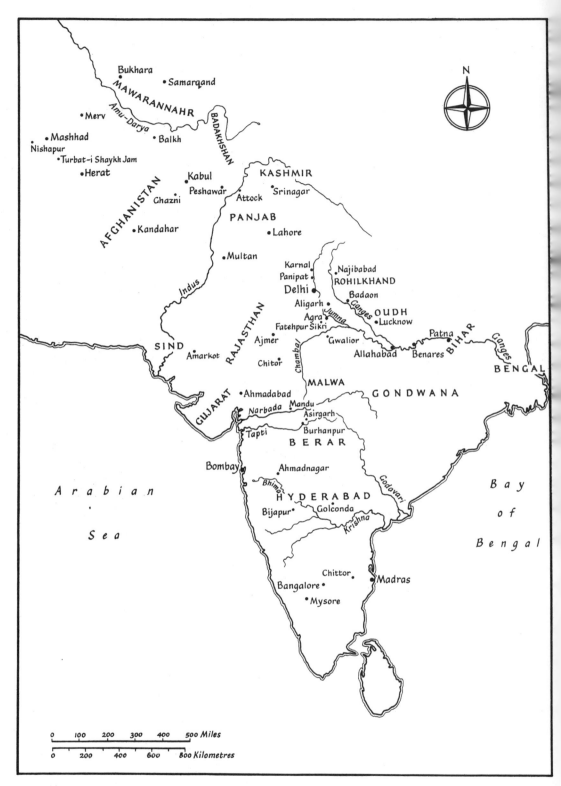

The World of the Mughuls

List of plates

Preface

In origin Turks from Central Asia, the Mughuls reigned in India from 1526 to 1858 and during the sixteenth and seventeenth centuries their favourite cities – Delhi, Agra, Fatehpur Sikri and Lahore – provided the setting for a brilliant court and a vigorous cultural life which was at least the equal of contemporary Isfahan under the Safavid Shahs or Istanbul under the Ottoman Sultans. The chapters which follow describe the fortunes of this great dynasty and its lavish patronage of the arts but, by way of introduction, the first chapter gives a brief account of Muslim rule in Delhi prior to the coming of the Mughuls.

In selecting illustrations to accompany the text the intention has been not only to demonstrate the profusion of skills which the craftsmen and artists of the Mughul court had at their disposal but also to provide, by means of contemporary miniatures, detailed vignettes of the daily life of the Mughul Emperors and the members of their entourage.

In the pages which follow the word *India* is used throughout in the pre-Independence sense of the whole sub-continent although the sub-title *Delhi, Agra and Fatehpur Sikri* precludes more than a passing reference to the Mughul buildings of Lahore, a favourite place of residence with both Akbar and Jahangir. It should be noted that the phrase *Old Delhi* is used invariably of Shahjahanabad, the city laid out by Shah Jahan beside the Red Fort, and never refers to the older foundations in the neighbourhood of the Qutb-Minar.

I wish to express my gratitude to all the museums, libraries and private collectors who have so generously granted permission for the reproduction of photographs of miniatures and other precious objects in their possession. I would also like to thank Mrs Mildred Archer of the India Office Library for her advice and assistance in locating material. I would like to thank the publishers, and in particular Miss Moira Johnston, for the enthusiasm and care with which they assembled the illustrations. Finally, I must record the debt which I owe to my wife for all her help and encouragement and in particular for the thankless task of reading through the manuscript.

Gavin Hambly
New Delhi
February 1968

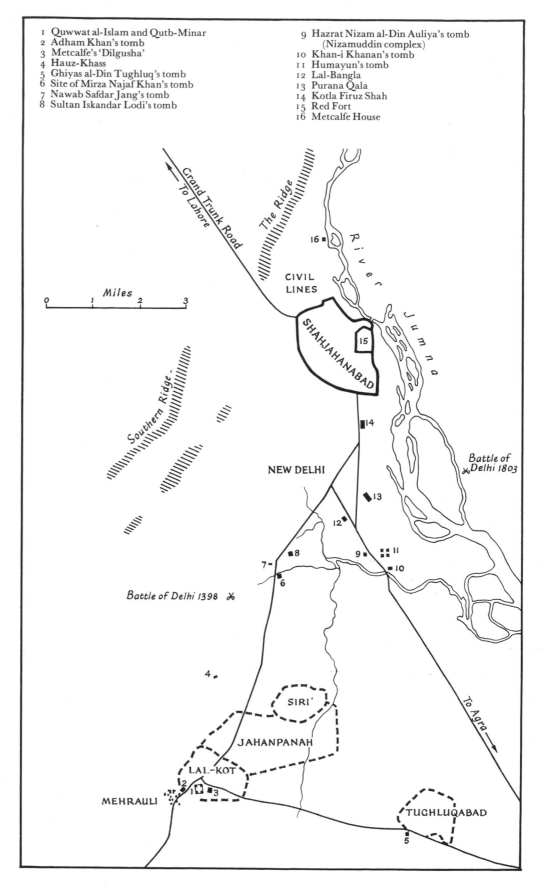

1 Quwwat al-Islam and Qutb-Minar
2 Adham Khan's tomb
3 Metcalfe's 'Dilgusha'
4 Hauz-Khass
5 Ghiyas al-Din Tughluq's tomb
6 Site of Mirza Najaf Khan's tomb
7 Nawab Safdar Jang's tomb
8 Sultan Iskandar Lodi's tomb
9 Hazrat Nizam al-Din Auliya's tomb
   (Nizamuddin complex)
10 Khan-i Khanan's tomb
11 Humayun's tomb
12 Lal-Bangla
13 Purana Qala
14 Kotla Firuz Shah
15 Red Fort
16 Metcalfe House

Miles
0   1   2   3

To Lahore
Grand Trunk Road

The Ridge

River Jumna

16

CIVIL
LINES

SHAHJAHANABAD

15

Southern Ridge

14

NEW DELHI

Battle of
Delhi 1803

13

12

8
7
6

9   11
     10

Battle of Delhi 1398

4

SIRI

To Agra

JAHANPANAH

LAL-KOT

2
1   3

MEHRAULI

TUGHLUQABAD

5

The Seven Cities of Delhi

12

Delhi under the Sultans

1206–1526

It cannot be said of Delhi, as it can of Rome or Istanbul, that its site was a natural location for the heart of an empire and it seems probable that its long pedigree as an imperial city was partly fortuitous. Although some of the most decisive events in the history of the sub-continent have taken place in the surrounding plains, the most probable explanation for Delhi's continuing importance from at least the thirteenth century up to the present time must surely be that, once the city had been established and had reached a certain size, it was sufficiently well placed to prevent any neighbouring city acting as a rival. The comparatively short periods when Agra and Fatehpur Sikri were the seats of Mughul government confirm rather than contradict the fact that once Delhi had come into existence as a political centre it was very hard to usurp its primacy. This is not to deny that Delhi's location possesses strategic significance but that significance would apply almost equally to any other city of a comparable size situated within a fifty-mile radius of it.

Delhi stands in the middle of a broad corridor of cultivation which links the Panjab to the Gangetic plain and which separates the north-eastern extremity of the Rajasthan desert and semi-desert region from the Himalayan foothills. This corridor is orientated from north-west to south-east, broadening out towards the latter where the Jumna, flowing from the north, meets the Chambal and then turns east to join the Ganges at Allahabad. Situated on the west bank of the Jumna, with the hills a hundred and fifty miles away, Delhi is cold in winter and hot in summer while the intervening seasons are mild and pleasant. Although lacking the fertility of Bengal, the rich agriculture of the Delhi countryside has always made its possession highly desirable to rulers requiring – as did all medieval rulers – a steady revenue from the land and wherever there is a regular supply of water, whether natural or provided by irrigation, the cultivator can obtain a good return for his labour, with only occasional fear of drought. To the south-east of Delhi especially, the Duab between the Jumna and the Ganges is fine farming land which even in medieval times supported a large rural population. In an age when, apart from transport by water, the bullock-cart was the only means of moving bulky goods, the prosperity of cities supporting a large population depended upon the proximity of easily-accessible supplies of grain and in the case of Delhi the Duab provided a granary close at hand.

Once Delhi had become established as a local centre of some importance it quickly acquired a strategic value from its position in the corridor between the Panjab and the Gangetic plain. A conqueror from the north-west, pausing at Delhi, could fan out his forces from the city, sending raiders south-east towards Bihar and Bengal or south towards Malwa and the Narbada. From Delhi he could hope to overawe the fortresses of Rajasthan while remaining close enough to the trans-Indus country to guard the Central Asian marches of the sub-continent and obtain reinforcements of men and horses from beyond the Hindu Kush.

Fig. 2 Silver *tanka* of Sultana Raziyeh minted at Laknauti (Bengal). *British Museum, London.* (*Actual size*)

Little is known about Delhi before the thirteenth century; its role as an imperial capital and as a centre of civilization coincides exactly with the succeeding six centuries of Muslim rule in north India. It is usual to date the history of Islam in the sub-continent from around AD 1000 when Sultan Mahmud, the ruler of a powerful military monarchy based on present-day Afghanistan and eastern Iran, began a series of raids on north-western India from his capital at Ghazni, south of Kabul. Muslims had made their way to India before then – Arab traders and missionaries had been drawn to the Malabar coast and Umayyid armies had penetrated Sind – but Mahmud of Ghazni's raids mark the real beginning of the story. For the Ghaznavids were Turks and the history of Islam in India as a dynamic force is, to a very considerable extent, the history of the Turks who were to display there, as in the lands further to the west, that characteristic Turkish ability to assimilate an alien culture while at the same time maintaining a dominant status as conquerors.

The Turks were not, however, the only architects of Indo-Islamic civilization. Close on their heels came the Persians, providing not only generations of soldiers, officials, scholars and artists but also weaving into the diverse and already sumptuous fabric of Indian civilization some of the most precious elements of Persian culture. There were others too, less conspicuous but nonetheless important – Pathans, Arabs, Mongols even – as well as those indigenous Muslims, converts from Hinduism, who made Islam in the sub-continent something far more eclectic and syncretistic than it had ever been in the Arabian desert or on the Central Asian steppes. Yet the leadership came from the Turks and the Persians, lured across the Indus by a combination of motives of which the quest for wealth and adventure was perhaps the chief. Without them neither the Muslim empires of medieval India nor what we recognize today as Indo-Islamic civilization would have taken the form they did.

Mahmud of Ghazni did not establish an empire in India; this was left to his successors who founded an eastern capital at Lahore early in the eleventh century. The Iranian territories which had been the core of Sultan Mahmud's kingdom had passed into the hands of a more powerful Turkish dynasty, the Seljuqs, who were to rule from Anatolia in the west to Kashgaria in the east, but they cared nothing for India. It was a local dynasty in Afghanistan, from the mountainous region of Ghur, east of Herat, which finally replaced the Ghaznavids as masters of north-western India and, like their predecessors, the Ghurids used Lahore as their base for extensive raiding further south. Both dynasties played a significant part in the patronage of Persian literature and left behind them in Afghanistan impressive monuments at Ghazni, Lashkar-i Bazar, Firuzkuh and elsewhere but little or nothing of their culture appears to have found its way to India where their role was primarily that of iconoclastic raiders.

Like other Islamic rulers the Ghurid Sultans employed as soldiers Turkish slaves (*mamluks*) brought from Central Asia and in course of time the most outstanding of these slaves were promoted through a graded hierarchy to the highest military commands, including the governership of provinces. By the thirteenth century a slave-soldiery had become a recognized institution in the eastern Islamic world and when in 1206 Sultan Muhammad of Ghur was assassinated, the ablest of his slave-commanders, Qutb al-Din Aibak, who had been appointed viceroy of the Delhi region as early as 1192, proclaimed himself Sultan and seized all the Indian territories of the Ghurids, although he was unable to secure possession of Afghanistan itself. The first of the so-called 'Slave-Kings' and the founder of the Delhi Sultanate, it was he who first made Delhi the capital of a Muslim kingdom in

India. The site of the city, Lal-Kot (cf. map page 12), was a Hindu foundation and it was here – probably during his years as viceroy – that he began building the congregational mosque known as the Quwwat al-Islam ('The Might of Islam'), using material taken from demolished Hindu temples in the vicinity without much effort being made to efface the original Hindu iconography. The Quwwat al-Islam was almost certainly the work of Hindu craftsmen and the overall effect of the building is Hindu rather than Muslim (cf. pl. 2). Close to it Qutb al-Din Aibak laid the foundations of the Qutb-Minar (cf. pl. 3), a combination of *minar* and commemorative tower, which is one of the finest surviving Muslim buildings in India. Only its base was complete when Qutb al-Din Aibak was killed in Lahore by a fall from his polo-pony in 1210 and it was left to his successor, Iltutmish (1211–36), to complete the greater part of this enormous structure. Despite decorative work which indicates indigenous Indian workmanship, the Qutb-Minar is, in fact, almost the last and certainly the grandest of a succession of Ghaznavid and Seljuqid funerary towers built in Afghanistan, Iran and Anatolia (e.g. at Ghazni, Gumbad-i Qabus, Ray, Varamin, Maragheh and Kayseri).

The greatest of Delhi's 'Slave-Kings', Iltutmish consolidated the Sultanate into a powerful military despotism, the logical outcome of the origin of its ruling class (a Turkish slave-soldiery), but also of its exposed position on the eastern extremity of the Islamic world, facing hostile Hindu principalities and threatened from the north-west throughout the thirteenth and much of the fourteenth century by the Mongol armies of Chingiz Khan and of the descendants of his second son, Chaghatai, who ruled Mawarannahr (the country lying between the rivers Amu-Darya and Syr-Darya and known in the nineteenth century as Russian Turkestan) as well as much of Afghanistan. The Mongol cataclysm in Central Asia, however, was not an unmitigated disaster for Indian Islam, whatever its effects elsewhere, for the rulers of Delhi not only acted as a rallying-point for opposition against further Mongol aggression but also offered sanctuary to thousands of refugees – including scholars, artists and craftsmen – fleeing from the Mongol holocaust in Iran and Mawarannahr. The rich cultural and spiritual life of thirteenth- and fourteenth-century Delhi owed much to this influx of people from such blighted centres of Islamic civilization as Nishapur, Merv, Herat, Balkh and Samarqand and the presence of these newcomers made Delhi seem – perhaps for the first time – a truly Muslim city.

The political institutions of the young state, however, remained unstable so long as the *amirs* (the military commanders) opposed the principle of hereditary succession to the throne. Any ruler who was to survive his first few months in power had to have a commanding personality, not only enough ruthlessness to usurp the throne but also sufficient ability to retain it.

Iltutmish died in 1236 and he named as his successor his daughter, Raziyeh, Delhi's only woman ruler. This romantic and accomplished figure reigned a mere four years until 1240 when she was killed at Kaithal in Karnal District and reputedly buried there. Yet in Old Delhi near the Kalan Masjid and not far from the Turkoman Gate there is an enclosure containing four graves, one of which is said to be hers.

Six years later Iltutmish's son, Nasir al-Din Mahmud (1246–66), ascended the throne and during the next twenty years every aspect of the administration became concentrated in the hands of his principal adviser, Ghiyas al-Din Balban, a former slave of Iltutmish who, on the death (or murder) of Nasir al-Din Mahmud, seized the throne and ruled with grim vigour for the following two decades (1266–87), consolidating the work of Iltutmish, priding himself on dealing justice to all and

Fig. 3 Gold *tanka* of Ala al-Din Muhammad Shah Khalji, minted at Delhi, A.H. 709 (A.D. 1309–10). *British Museum, London. (Actual size)*

1 Sovereigns and princes of the House of Timur. Painting on cotton by Mir Sayyid Ali or Abd-us-Samad (?), c. 1555, and altered in the early 17th century. In the pavilion (*seated from left to right*) are Shah Jahan, Jahangir, Akbar and Humayun. Seated on the extreme right is Timur's fourth son and successor, Shah Rukh. On the left of the pavilion the five figures seated in a row are Babur and his ancestors, Shaykh Umar, Abu Said, Sultan Muhammad and Miranshah, Timur's third son. *British Museum, London.* (107.5 × 111.5 cm.)

2 Quwwat al-Islam Masjid, Delhi, built by Qutb al-Din Aibak between 1193 and 1197.

3 Qutb-Minar, Delhi, begun by Qutb al-Din Aibak and completed by his son-in-law and successor, Iltutmish (1211–36). It was later repaired by Firuz Shah Tughluq and Iskandar Lodi.

4 Alai Darwaza, Delhi, the sole surviving gateway to the Quwwat al-Islam Masjid built by the Khalji Sultan, Ala al-Din Muhammad Shah, in 1311.

sundry with a harsh, even hand, and riding out again and again to battle with the Mongols in the Panjab. During his reign, much to the disgust of the *ulama*, the monarchy began to acquire a formal splendour approaching that of the ancient kings of Iran and it was at Balban's court that the greatest of India's Persian poets, Amir Khusru Dihlavi (1253–1325), first established his reputation. Yet life in Delhi under the aging tyrant, an octogenarian at the time of his death, must have been fearful and uncertain. With the accession of his grandson, Muizz al-Din Kayqubad (1287–90), a reaction set in and Delhi became a city devoted to the pursuit of pleasure, with courtesans in the shadow of every wall and fair figures displaying their wares on every balcony.

No buildings of any artistic merit built between the death of Iltutmish in 1236 and the seizure of the throne in 1290 by the Khaljis, who thus ended the rule of the 'Slave-Kings', have survived in Delhi. Presumably the constant threat from the Mongols, which necessitated the maintenance of a large army on a continuous war-footing, meant that extensive building-projects were beyond the resources of the state and it was only during the next thirty years of Khalji rule (1290–1320), a period of stability, strong government and expanding revenue, that really considerable funds could be allotted to the expansion and embellishment of the capital. Of the three principal Khalji Sultans the first, Jalal al-Din Firuz Shah, reigned for a brief six years (1290–6). He was then murdered by his nephew, Ala al-Din Muhammad Shah (1296–1316), the greatest of Delhi's pre-Mughul rulers and an empire-builder whose expeditions into the south pointed the way to Akbar's and Aurangzeb's later ambitions of sovereignty over all India. His son, Qutb al-Din Mubarak Shah (1316–20), inherited his father's pride and alone among Indian rulers appropriated the Caliph's title of *amir al muminin* ('Commander of the Faithful') but he lacked ability and his assassination marked the extinction of this short-lived brilliant dynasty.

Ala al-Din Muhammad Shah's conquests provided resources which enabled him to indulge in building on a scale impossible for his predecessors. He first turned to the Quwwat al-Islam mosque at Lal-Kot for a preliminary attempt at grandiose planning, enlarged it to cover twice the area it occupied as a result of Iltutmish's additions, enclosed it within a new wall broken by four gateways of which only one – the magnificent Alai Darwaza (cf. pls. 4, 10) – still remains, and began a new *minar* (of which the first storey alone was completed) which was to be twice the size of the Qutb-Minar. To the south-west of the original mosque he founded a *madraseh* (a Muslim theological college) and it was here too that he built his tomb.

Not content with Lal-Kot, which was becoming too cramped for the capital of a fast-expanding empire, he founded the second of Delhi's cities at nearby Siri, now marked only by crumbling walls, and it was to provide water for this new centre that he constructed the reservoir known today as Hauz-Khass but then as Hauz-i Alai (cf. map, page 12).

The Khalji style differs strikingly from that of the early thirteenth century and some of its most distinctive features, such as its decorative mouldings, pointed horse-shoe arches and spear-headed fringes on the underside of the arches – all of which are to be found on the Alai Darwaza (cf. pl. 10) – are also characteristic of Seljuq workmanship in Anatolia. It was during the period of Khalji rule in Delhi that the Seljuq Sultanate succumbed to Mongol pressure and it is possible that a few craftsmen and master-builders may have come from Anatolia to India as refugees.

In 1320 the Khaljis gave way to the Tughluqs and the harsh puritanical character of the founder of the new dynasty, Ghiyas al-Din Tughluq, is well illustrated by Tughluqabad, the third city of Delhi, which he built several miles

2

3

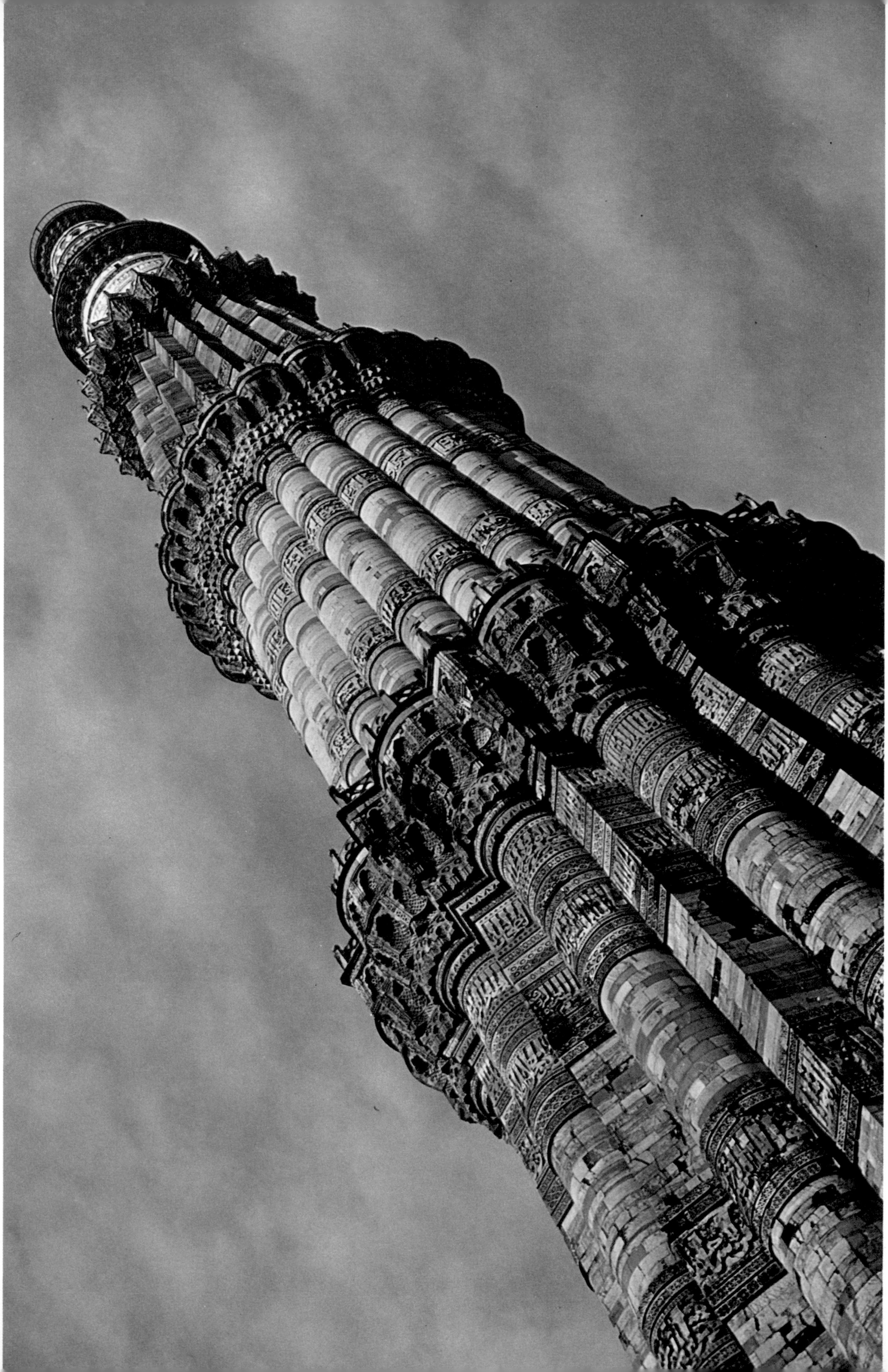

6

Fig. 4 Gold *dinar* of Muhammad ibn Tughluq, minted at Delhi, A.H. 726 (A.D. 1325–6). *British Museum, London.* (*Actual size*)

5 Part of the tomb of the Chishti saint, Hazrat Nizam al-Din Auliya (1236–1325), Delhi. The original tomb has disappeared and the present structure dates from the reign of Akbar. Behind is the Jamaat Khana Masjid begun by Khizr Khan, son of Ala al-Din Muhammad Shah, and completed in 1325.

6 The tomb of Ghiyas al-Din Tughluq (1320–5), Tughluqabad, Delhi.

7 Bara-Gumbad, Lodi Gardens (formerly the Lady Willingdon Park), Delhi. Built in 1494 during the reign of Iskandar Lodi, it is not known for whom this tomb was constructed. On the left is a small mosque.

8 Bara-Gumbad Masjid, Lodi Gardens, Delhi. Detail of the plaster-work.

9 Miniature: Abul Fazl presenting the second volume of the *Akbarnameh* to Akbar. Painting by Govardhan, c. 1602–5. *Akbarnameh. Chester Beatty Library, Dublin,* Ms. 3 fo. 176b–177. (24 × 13.5 cm.)

due east of Lal-Kot with a cyclopean citadel designed primarily to withstand renewed Mongol attacks. Ghiyas al-Din's short reign of five years (1320–5) ended in a misadventure in which his son and successor, Muhammad (1325–51), probably had a hand, but under the new Sultan medieval Delhi reached its apogee of splendour. The much-travelled Moroccan, Ibn Battuta, who lived in the city between 1335 and 1342, wrote that it was then the largest city in India and the Muslim East, with fortifications (presumably those of Tughluqabad) equalled only by those of Mosul on the Tigris. Very accurately, he defined Delhi as consisting of four adjacent towns (cf. map, page 12): Lal-Kot, the old city, formerly Hindu and captured by the Ghurids in 1193; Siri, founded by Ala al-Din Khalji; Tughluqabad, founded by Ghiyas al-Din Tughluq; and Jahanpanah, a new centre built by Sultan Muhammad himself and lying between Lal-Kot and Siri. The reason why Sultan Muhammad abandoned Tughluqabad for Jahanpanah is uncertain but it was probably connected with a failure in the water-supply of the former. Ibn Battuta speaks of a plan to enclose all four cities within one single wall but the project had to be abandoned because of the cost. The most important building to have survived from Sultan Muhammad's reign is his father's tomb, a simple square structure in red sandstone and marble, capped by a dome in the style of Il-Khanid Iran, placed upon a high, well-fortified platform outside the southern ramparts of Tughluqabad and originally surrounded by a reservoir of water (cf. pl. 6).

In his account of Delhi, Ibn Battuta described in detail the vanished palace of Sultan Muhammad, the stern ceremonial enforced at his court and the terror which he inspired among his subjects. There is no doubt, however, that the ruling class of *amirs*, together with their followers, were – even by medieval standards – peculiarly turbulent and the Sultan's savage despotism betrayed his determination to maintain his authority at all costs.

The violent character of political life in the Delhi Sultanate calls for some explanation. Those Turkish warriors who, some time prior to the establishment of Muslim rule in India, had carved out kingdoms for themselves in the Middle East had been confronted there by well-established patterns of political conduct and administrative practice. These were theoretically Muslim but largely Persian in spirit and manipulated by a Persian or semi-Persianized bureaucracy thoroughly imbued with pre-Islamic Persian concepts of kingship and statecraft, to which the newcomers had quickly responded. In India, however, the situation was very different. There the Turks found themselves living among a majority of infidel subjects while, during the greater part of the thirteenth century and the early part of the fourteenth century, the presence of the Mongols on the north-west frontier cut them off from the traditional centres of Islamic civilization in Iran and Mawarannahr which, in any case, the Mongols had all but obliterated. Thus the Delhi Sultanate became frontier-country and its ruling class displayed all the recklessness, ruthlessness and unconventionality which at all times characterizes the pioneer. This lack of traditional restraints is indirectly confirmed by Ibn Battuta when he remarks:

'A man is honoured in that country [Delhi] according to what may be seen of his actions, conduct, and zeal, since no one knows anything of his family or lineage.'[1]

According to Ibn Battuta, Sultan Muhammad was distinguished both for his generosity and for the freedom with which he shed blood and there can be no doubt that his brilliant gifts were offset by a waywardness bordering upon insanity. By 1327 he had acquired such an irrational loathing for Delhi and its inhabitants that he forcibly transferred his capital to Daulatabad in the Deccan, causing great suffering to those who were compelled to make the long trek southwards. The experiment failed and Delhi was in due course restored to favour but 1327 stands out as the first *gardi* in Delhi's long history of disasters. To most of its citizens Sultan Muhammad's death must have come as a relief and the succession of his cousin, Firuz Shah Tughluq (1351–88), introduced an interlude of relative peace and prosperity.

Firuz Shah Tughluq was a builder on a grand scale. Apart from the canals, hunting-lodges and pavilions which he constructed in the countryside around Delhi (a sure sign of tranquil times) he repaired the Qutb-Minar, cleared the then derelict Hauz-Khass and erected on its banks a spacious *madraseh* enclosing his tomb. The *madraseh* rapidly developed as the foremost centre of Muslim learning in the sub-continent and around it grew up a popular suburb. The nobility were quick to emulate their master's passion for architecture and from this reign date the Begampuri Masjid and the Khirki Masjid in Jahanpanah, the Kalan Masjid in Nizamuddin, and the Kalan Masjid in Old Delhi. Firuz Shah Tughluq was also the first ruler of Delhi to abandon the Lal-Kot area for a new site several miles to the north-east on the west bank of the Jumna. The stark remains of this fifth city of Delhi, known today as Kotla Firuz Shah, convey little idea of the splendour of the original Firuzabad.

The Tughluq dynasty did not long survive Firuz Shah's death in 1388. Within a decade it was swept aside by the advance of a Central Asian conqueror even more savage than Chingiz Khan. Timur, a Barlas Turk from Mawarannahr, invaded India in 1398 and entered Delhi after defeating the Tughluqid army in a pitched battle near the site of the present Safdar Jang airport. For days the city was systematically plundered and many of its inhabitants, especially the women and the craftsmen, were eventually transported to Samarqand. This holocaust ended the period when Delhi was the undisputed centre of Muslim civilization in the sub-continent and for the next century and a quarter the Sultanate languished while new centres of Muslim power and culture emerged at Jaunpur, Mandu, Gaur, Ahmadabad, Burhanpur, Bidar and Gulbarga.

Delhi's fate during those twelve decades is soon told. The period immediately following Timur's invasion was one of utter anarchy. The city itself, its environs and the surrounding countryside had been stripped of all their resources and the Sultanate survived as little more than a name. Then in 1414 a change came for the better when the city was seized by Timur's governor in Multan, Khizr Khan, who was content to rule, not as Sultan, but as viceroy of Timur's son, Shah Rukh. Khizr Khan claimed the Prophet Muhammad as an ancestor and hence he and his three successors are known as the Sayyid dynasty. The most that can be said in their favour is that, reigning in unquiet times, they managed to preserve the independence of Delhi from ambitious rivals and began the work of reconstruction. Not one of them, however, was of more than average ability and the petty kingdom of the last of the line, Ala al-Din Alam Shah, prompted a wag to compose the Persian couplet:

Shahanshahi Shah Alam
*az Dihli ta Palam**

In 1451 he resigned his throne to an Afghan chieftain of the Lodi tribe, Bahlul Khan, and withdrew to Badaon where he passed his final years in the quiet pursuit of pleasure.

Fig. 5 A billon coin of Bahlul Lodi, minted at Delhi, A.H. 865 (A.D. 1460–1). *British Museum, London. (Actual size)*

*The lines turn on a pun in the Sultan's name: 'The dominion (shahanshahi) of the King of the World (Shah Alam) extends from Delhi to Palam', a village in the neighbourhood of Delhi and now the site of its international airport.

By the middle of the fifteenth century the Afghans had become the dominant military element in northern India which they entered, not like the Turks as bands of warriors, but as closely-knit tribal and clan units. As warlike as the Turks and just as turbulent, their tribal loyalties made them less susceptible to discipline. Once in possession of Delhi, Bahlul Khan (1451–89) fought tirelessly to incorporate the Panjab and the Jumna-Ganges Duab into his little kingdom while the conquests of his brilliant son, Sultan Iskandar (1489–1517), enabled him to restore to the Sultanate much of its old glory. The third Lodi ruler, Sultan Ibrahim, however, lacked the conciliatory ways of his father and grandfather in dealing with his tribal supporters and it was partly due to their alienation, as well as to the fact that his Mughul opponents were better led and better equipped, that he was defeated by Babur at Panipat in 1526.

The exact location of Sayyid and Lodi Delhi is far from certain. It may have been centred on Kotla Firuz Shah (cf. map, page 12) or, alternatively, to the south and close to the site where the Purana Qala was soon to be built and where there may have already been a smaller fort constructed during the fifteenth century. Judging from the surviving quantity of masonry dating from this period there may also have been a sizeable concentration of population living in the vicinity of what is now the Lady Willingdon Park (generally known as the Lodi Gardens). The Sayyid dynasty never possessed adequate resources for much building but the countryside around Delhi is still strewn with a large number of anonymous buildings in the Lodi style of which some, especially the fine tombs in the Lady Willingdon Park (cf. pls. 7, 8, 11), combine harmonious proportions and decorative work of a very high quality with a feeling of monumental strength reminiscent, outside India, of the best Seljuq architecture of two centuries earlier. Tilework appears to have been used extensively in the decoration of some of the more important Lodi tombs and, although it is unlikely that the craftsmen of this period approached the skill in tiling of their Timurid contemporaries in Khurasan and Mawarannahr, it is unfortunate that no example of a large tiled surface has survived from Lodi times to make a comparison.

The Lodi rulers and their courtiers built both square and octagonal-shaped tombs, their most ambitious undertaking being the octagonal tomb of Sultan Iskandar which was constructed within a walled and semi-fortified garden, thereby providing a link between the fortress-like mausoleum of Ghiyas al-Din Tughluq and the garden-tombs of Mughul times.

Sultan Iskandar possessed greater resources than any ruler of Delhi between Firuz Shah Tughluq and Sher Shah (1540–5), and his comparative affluence among fifteenth-century rulers may have influenced his decision in 1504 to establish his court at Agra, a hundred and twenty miles south of Delhi on the west bank of the Jumna. His choice of an alternative residence to Delhi inaugurated that period of nearly a century and a half when the two cities uneasily shared the status of twin-capitals.

1526–1556

Babur's victory at Panipat in 1526 ended the Delhi Sultanate and established in its place the Mughul Empire which, in name at least, was to survive until 1858.

The new conqueror of Delhi was just over forty. Born in 1483, he had spent the first twenty-one years of his stormy career fighting for his father's Central Asian principality of Farghana and for possession of Samarqand. For a further twenty-two years, between 1504 and 1526, he had been ruler of Kabul. It was therefore only between 1526 and his death in 1530 that he played any part on the Indian stage and those four brief years gave him little opportunity to leave an enduring mark. Racially he was a Turk with only a thin stream of Mongol blood in his veins so that the term 'Mughul' by which he and his descendants are known in India is really a misnomer. In Persian the word *mughul*, always highly pejorative among the civilized inhabitants of Iran or Mawarannahr, simply means a Mongol but it is clear from his own writings that Babur regarded himself as a Turk (Chaghatai Turkish was his mother-tongue) and despised the heathen or semi-Islamicized 'Mughuls' of 'Mughulistan' (the name given by the inhabitants of Mawarannahr to the country north-east of the Pamirs and the Syr-Darya). Although he was descended on his mother's side from Chingiz Khan's second son, Chaghatai, it is clear that to Babur this Mongol lineage meant less than his paternal ancestry which linked him with the great Turkish conqueror, Timur.

Central Asia in the fifteenth century consisted of a proliferation of unstable principalities engaged in almost continuous conflict with each other yet somehow capable of supporting a literary and artistic life of dazzling virtuosity, in which Persian and Turkish elements harmonized to produce a synthesis which, when transplanted into Indian soil, would become a dominant feature of Mughul civilization. Surprisingly enough, neither Samarqand, the former capital of the Timurid empire and still a glittering prize for Babur and his contemporaries, nor Bukhara, now beginning to sink into obscurantist torpor, served as a focal point for this brilliant cultural efflorescence. This was provided by the city of Herat in north-western Afghanistan which, at the height of its glory in the last decades of the century under the rule of Babur's distant relative, Sultan Husayn Bayqara, sheltered Bihzad and the Herat School of miniature-painters, Jami the last great Persian classical poet, and Mir Ali Shir Navai who did so much to make Chaghatai Turkish the polished literary vehicle which Babur himself used later as the language of his memoirs. Looking back to the lifetime of Sultan Husayn Bayqara, Babur recalled the period with obvious nostalgia:

'His was a wonderful Age; in it Khurasan, and Herat above all, was full of learned and matchless men. Whatever the work a man took up, he aimed and aspired at bringing that work to perfection.'[2]

The civilization of Herat was to leave an indelible stamp upon the warriors and courtiers who accompanied Babur into India and contemporary sources, reinforced

10 Alai Darwaza, Delhi. Detail of the arch.

11 Bara-Gumbad, Lodi Gardens, Delhi. Detail of the doorway.

12 The tomb of Muhammad Shah (1434–44), third ruler of the Sayyid dynasty, Lodi Gardens, Delhi.

13 The tomb of Humayun, Delhi, built by his widow, Hamida Banu Begum, during the reign of Akbar.

14 The tomb of Humayun, Delhi. Marble screen.

16

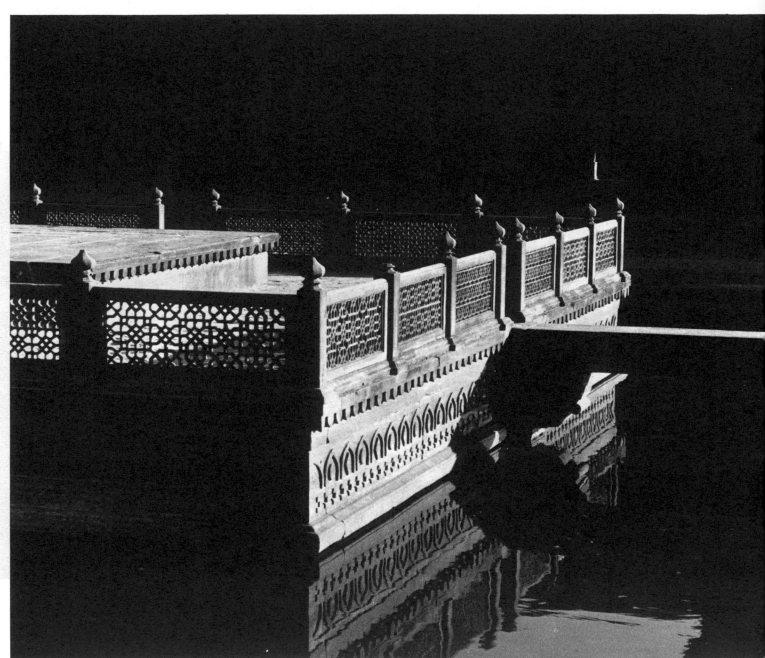

18

by a wealth of information contained in the miniatures, have preserved a vivid image of the type of men they were. Turks for the most part, boasting high-sounding genealogies from the conquering tribes and clans of Inner Asia, yet steeped in Persian traditions of culture and refinement, they delighted in war and the chase, in their skill with bow and scimitar and polo-stick, and in the possession of fine weapons, horses and hunting-falcons. Out of the saddle they would turn from watching wrestlers and fighting-rams to the quiet of the chess-board or the painter's *atelier*, and from drinking bouts with courtesans and bibulous poets to the company of scholars, *shaykhs* and dervishes. Patrons of art and learning they were themselves often poets in Persian or Chaghatai Turkish in their own right, amateur painters or calligraphers, singers or instrumentalists even as well as lovers of music. This was an age when it was no disgrace for a prince or his officers to handle a brush or a pen as dexterously as a sword, an age which combined – however incongruously – exquisite courtesy and the strict regulation of personal relationships with the most reckless conduct and the most unrestrained excess. Lovers of palaces and gilded tents, indulging in fine clothing and rich accoutrements, collectors of books and paintings, avid for every new luxury, this generation of conquerors retained enough of that wandering spirit of their Central Asian ancestors to entice them from the mountains and steppes of their homeland to lives of adventure in lands as remote as Bengal and the Deccan.

Given a choice, Babur would probably have preferred to remain north of the Hindu Kush, fighting his Timurid and Chaghatai kinsfolk for the possession of Samarqand, but it was his misfortune that he had as a contemporary an even greater warrior than himself, the Uzbek conqueror, Muhammad Shaybani, a direct descendant of Chingiz Khan through the latter's eldest son, Juji (cf. fig. 6).

It was Muhammad Shaybani who compelled Babur to flee from Mawarannahr in 1504 and to carve out a new principality for himself in Afghanistan. Even there he did not feel entirely safe until after 1510 when Muhammad Shaybani was defeated and killed in battle near Merv by Shah Ismail, founder of the Safavid dynasty in Iran. Babur made a last reckless attempt to seize Samarqand from the Uzbeks in 1511 but after a brief occupation of the city he was beaten off by Ubaydullah Khan, Muhammad Shaybani's nephew. Even the active support of Shah Ismail failed to dislodge the Uzbeks a second time and Babur withdrew finally to Kabul. Henceforth, he turned his attention southwards – to India.

Between 1512 and 1526 Babur more than once descended towards the Indus valley but though his thoughts often turned to the conquest of Delhi he lacked the resources to mount a sufficiently large expedition. The steady decline of Sultan Ibrahim's popularity was, however, a factor working strongly in favour of a change of regime and in 1526 Babur seized the opportunity of uniting all his followers in an adventure which, if successful, would offer them boundless wealth. At Panipat his guns and his skill as a commander brought him a well-deserved victory which was to change the course of Indian history.

After the battle Babur sent his eldest son, Humayun, to seize Sultan Ibrahim's household and treasure at Agra while he himself advanced on Delhi. Although he was an inveterate sightseer there is no evidence that the imperial city greatly impressed him. He toured most of its principal monuments but, among Indian buildings, reserved his enthusiasm for the Man Mandir, the palace at Gwalior of Maharaja Man Singh (1486–1516). As soon as he had seen all he wanted he withdrew to a boat on the Jumna with some of his boon-companions and indulged in an evening of drinking *arak* before moving on to Agra a few days later. Very few buildings in Delhi, incidentally, can be attributed with any certainty to the second

Fig. 6 Miniature: The Uzbek conqueror of Mawarannahr, Muhammad Shaybani (*d.* 1510). By an unknown painter of the Herat School. *Bequest of Cora Timken Burnett, 1957, Metropolitan Museum of Art, New York.*

15 Buland Darwaza, the gateway to the Jami Masjid, Fatehpur Sikri. This enormous structure, one hundred and thirty-four feet high, was built to commemorate the capture of the fort of Asirgarh in 1601.

16 Fatehpur Sikri. The second courtyard, looking towards the school for the children of the imperial household and (*right*) the Panch Mahal.

17 Fatehpur Sikri. Ornamental tank in the second courtyard.

18 Fatehpur Sikri. Rooftop view of the Jodh Bai Palace, looking towards the Jami Masjid.

quarter of the sixteenth century but one notable exception is the well-proportioned mosque and square tomb-chamber (the latter containing some elegant plaster-work) of Shaykh Fazlullah Jamal Khan in Mehrauli.

Babur seems to have regarded his Indian conquests with qualified enthusiasm. His active and inquisitive mind found much to investigate and wonder at in India – especially the flora and fauna – but the country itself had little appeal and in his memoirs he frankly admits his dislike for it.

'Hindustan is a country of few charms. Its people have no good looks; of social intercourse, paying and receiving visits there is none; of genius and capacity none; of manners none; in handicraft and work there is no form or symmetry, method or quality; there are no good horses, no good dogs, no grapes, no musk-melons or first-rate fruits, no ice or cold water, no good bread or cooked food in the bazaars, no hot-baths, no colleges, no candles, torches or candlesticks . . .

There are no running-waters in their gardens or residences. These residences have no charm, air, regularity or symmetry . . .

Pleasant things in Hindustan are that it is a large country and has masses of gold and silver . . .

Another good thing in Hindustan is that it has unnumbered and endless workmen of every kind.' [3]

Babur was particularly depressed to find in India no gardens such as he had known in Central Asia and had himself laid out in Kabul. Not long after his arrival in Agra, therefore, he selected a site across the river from the town where, despite his initial mistrust of its potentialities, he soon had the ground cleared, a well dug and a bath-house constructed. This was followed by a tank and a pavilion, and soon a Persian garden began to take shape, reminding him of his northern home.

'Then', he wrote in his memoirs, 'in that charmless and disorderly Hind, plots of gardens were seen laid out with order and symmetry, with suitable borders and parterres in every corner, and in every border rose and narcissus in perfect arrangement.' [4]

Babur would plan a garden with the same care as a campaign. He would turn aside from the line of march to pick an unfamiliar flower. He had a keen eye for natural beauty of every kind and his memoirs abound with references to new plants, birds or animals. Similarly, although so much of his life was occupied in warfare and physical exertion, he took an unaffected pleasure in the company of artists and writers, approaching them not in the spirit of a princely Maecenas but as one of themselves, with serious literary contributions to his credit. Brave, good-humoured and relatively humane by the standards of the age, Babur's complex but attractive personality combined a fine sense of taste and style with boyish gaiety and the obvious virtues of the soldier and the ruler. It is tempting to see his legacy to his successors in their artistic sensitivity and passion for beautiful things, and in their articulate patronage of Persian and, later, indigenous Indian culture, as well as in their personal courage and the vigour with which they extended their possessions in India.

Babur's successor, Humayun, was only twenty-two at the time of his father's death and he lacked both the experience and the tough fibre necessary to consolidate a new dynasty. Hence the next decade saw the steady erosion of Mughul authority in northern India in the face of the determined hostility of the Afghans already settled there, many of whom had been closely allied with the dispossessed Lodis. The leadership in this counter-attack was provided by an

Afghan chieftain of genius from Bihar who first expelled Humayun's troops from the Gangetic plain, then compelled them to vacate Delhi, and finally, around 1540, drove them out of the Panjab and proclaimed himself Sher Shah Sur.

Between 1540 and 1545 Sher Shah was master of northern India from the east bank of the Indus and the foothills of the Himalayas to Malwa and distant Assam. Historians have a habit of referring to this period as one of Afghan usurpation but the phrase is a misleading one since to contemporaries it was Babur and Humayun who seemed usurpers and when Sher Shah drove the Mughuls back beyond the Indus it must have looked as if he was doing no more than restoring the Afghan *raj* which Babur had wrenched from the Lodi Sultans.

Sher Shah was one of the most able rulers India has ever seen and it is no exaggeration to say that the imperial systems of Mughul and British times were constructed upon foundations of his making. During a brief reign of five years he made his impact felt upon almost every aspect of government and administration. Most important of all, he understood the necessity of defining properly the obligations of the cultivators towards the state so that his innovations in the assessment and collection of the land revenue established a pattern which strong governments were to follow for the next four centuries.

Sher Shah's Delhi, once again the capital of a great empire, was bounded on the east by the Jumna and extended northwards as far as Kotla Firuz Shah close to which the Kabul Gate of Sher Shah's city still stands in lonely isolation. Its southern limit must have been the enormous citadel known as the Purana Qala beyond which gardens stretched as far as the Nizamuddin area, the traditional burial-ground of the Muslim nobility. The ruler's residence, the treasury and the seat of government were all located in the Purana Qala itself (cf. pl. 122). It is impossible to know what the interior of this great fort with its three imposing gateways was like at that time since hardly anything remains inside the crumbling walls apart from Sher Shah's mosque, one of Delhi's most impressive monuments which, taken with Sher Shah's mausoleum at Sasaram in Bihar, fitly commemorates Afghanistan's greatest son. Delhi has certainly known no greater master. Less ambiguous than Akbar, less devious than Aurangzeb, his imperial vision and his ability to translate that vision into constructive action place him in the front rank of India's statesmen.

Sher Shah died in 1545 but for the next nine years his kingdom survived almost intact in the hands of his son, Islam Shah, an active, able ruler whose virtues were marred by a capricious, unconciliatory nature ill-suited to governing Afghan chieftains who looked to their sovereign as a *primus inter pares*. After his death in 1554 the Sur dynasty rapidly collapsed in bloodshed and the return of the Mughuls a year later confirmed the end of Afghan rule in northern India, although in the heyday of the Mughul Empire individual Afghans would play a glorious part in the military annals of the times and in the middle of the eighteenth century would once again ride into Delhi as conquerors.

When, in the late seventeenth century, the Emperor Aurangzeb was playing off the frontier tribes against each other the Pashtu poet, Khushal Khan Khattak, recalled nostalgically the great days passed for ever:

> 'And yet Pathans, in all their deeds
> Are better than the Moguls;
> But unanimity they lack,
> And there's the pity of it.

Fig. 7 Silver rupee of Sher Shah Sur, minted at Shergarh, A.H. 949 (A.D. 1542–3). *British Museum London.* (*Actual size*)

> I hear talk of Sultan Bahlol,
> Also of Sher Shah Sur:
> They were Pathans who won renown
> As Emperors in Hind.
>
> For six or seven generations
> They ruled in such a way
> That all the people were amazed
> At their accomplishments.
>
> Either they were another kind
> From these Pathans today,
> Or else it is by God's command
> That things have reached this pass.'[5]

Fig. 8 Silver *tanka* of Humayun, minted at Delhi, A.H. 962 (A.D. 1554–5). *British Museum, London.* (*Actual size*)

In Khushal Khan's verse there is bitter regret for opportunities thrown away, yet in the history of Delhi the exploits of the Afghans provided at least two splendid interludes still commemorated by the fine mausoleums of the Lodi period and by the fortifications of the Purana Qala, impressive even in decay.

When Humayun was expelled from the Panjab by Sher Shah he presumably hoped to retain what was left of his father's possessions in Afghanistan but in this he was thwarted by his younger brother, Mirza Kamran, ruler of Kabul, and within a matter of months had passed from being the ruler of northern India to a hunted fugitive. It was during this desperate period of his life that his Persian wife, Hamida Begum, a native of Turbat-i Shaykh Jam in Khurasan, gave birth to the future emperor Akbar at Amarkot in Sind (1542). After experiencing both danger and privation in the arid country west of the Indus Humayun eventually made his way to Iran where Shah Ismail's successor, Shah Tahmasb (1524–76), provided him with enough troops to recapture Kandahar, thereby loosening Mirza Kamran's grip on Kabul although it took almost another decade before this formidable rival could be eliminated. Once he was securely re-established in Kabul it was inevitable that the squabbles of Islam Shah's feeble successors should tempt him to try his hand once more in India and in 1555 he had little difficulty in regaining Delhi. Even though he was restored to his kingdom after fifteen years of wandering, ill-fortune continued to dog his footsteps and in the following January, at the age of only forty-eight, he was killed by falling down the steps of his library in his haste to obey the muezzin's call to prayer.

Historians have been somewhat less than generous to Humayun, for the main charge levelled against him – that he lost his throne – applies equally to Babur. Indeed, in a number of ways the careers of father and son bear a striking resemblance. Both were compelled to abandon their kingdoms – Babur to Muhammad Shaybani and Humayun to Sher Shah – but both survived their formidable adversaries. Both suffered from the treachery or neglect of relatives who might have succoured them. Both turned to Iran for assistance, made some sort of submission to the Safavid Shahs, and were then guilty of a breach of faith. Both too were genial, easy-going men in a brutal age, sensible and civilized, and capable of arousing strong feelings of loyalty. Unlike Babur, however, Humayun was a feeble commander, lacked any flair for leadership and was notorious for his bad luck. Percival Spear has called him 'a Mughul Stuart perhaps, a fair and fatal king'[6] and the analogy is an apt one. His one positive achievement lay in the field of painting, where his devotion to the early Safavid School, acquired during his stay in Iran, led him to recruit Persian painters of real merit to accompany him

40

back to India. These exiles were to lay the foundations of the Mughul style which, half a century later, would emerge from its Persian chrysalis as an indigenous achievement in which Indian elements would blend harmoniously with the traditions of Iran and Central Asia.

Humayun's tomb (cf. pl. 13), with its immense dome of white marble which dominates the landscape of Delhi towards the south-east, is a monument to the devotion of Hamida Begum, his widow, who supervised its construction during the early years of the following reign. It also marks the beginning of a major development in the history of Indo-Islamic architecture, being the first of a succession of monumental garden-tombs built in the Mughul period of which the most important are the nearby tomb of the Khan-i Khanan in south Nizamuddin (now stripped of its facing-stones), the highly idiosyncratic mausoleum of Akbar at Sikandra outside Agra (cf. pls. 39, 40) and that of Jahangir at Shahdara across the Ravi from Lahore, the tomb of Itimad al-Dowleh (cf. pl. 53) and the Taj Mahal at Agra (cf. pl. 58), the tomb of Aurangzeb's wife at Aurangabad and Nawab Safdar Jang's tomb in Delhi (cf. fig. 21, page 149).

Standing on a large square platform of red sandstone, the first and perhaps the most abiding impression which Humayun's tomb leaves upon the visitor is one of size; compared with the surviving monuments of pre-Mughul Delhi it is enormous and the effect is enhanced by the skilful juxtaposition of white marble and red sandstone which relieves the facade of any suggestion of monotony. The whole conception – notwithstanding the typically Indian *chhatris* on the roof – exemplifies the alien Persian element which was to make itself felt in the majority of Mughul buildings constructed during the next three centuries. In both spirit and substance Humayun's tomb is Persian architecture, not quite of the best but certainly of a very high standard, beautifully proportioned and with an instinctive feeling for spatial effect – especially the interior where the central octagonal tomb-chamber is reminiscent of the superb fourteenth-century mausoleum of the Il-Khan Uljaytu at Sultaniyeh in north-western Iran, a building which both Humayun and Hamida Begum may well have visited in the course of their stay at Shah Tahmasb's court. Also reminiscent of Persian prototypes (in this case, the so-called 'Tatar' domes evolved in Il-Khanid times and brought to perfection by the Timurids) is the fine double dome – a Persian invention here used for the first time in the sub-continent – which must rank, with that of the Khan-i Khanan's tomb, as the best-proportioned dome in India. That Iran should have provided the main inspiration for this great mausoleum is not, however, surprising for Hamida Begum was a Persian herself and from the province of Khurasan where, throughout the preceding century, the finest Persian architecture had been located.

1556–1605

At the time of Humayun's death his eldest son, Akbar, was only fourteen and the Mughul re-conquest of the Panjab and the country around Delhi had yet to be consolidated. No sooner was Humayun's death made public than a formidable anti-Mughul coalition (consisting mainly of Afghan elements) came into being and it was only after a second fiercely-fought engagement at Panipat (1556) that Mughul control over northern India was finally established. Thereafter, for the next half century until his death in 1605, Akbar pursued a policy of vigorous expansion until his empire bestraddled the greater part of the sub-continent north of the Godavari. Although able to prove himself as warlike as any of his ancestors, he also developed into a statesman of vision whose concept of empire was sufficiently enlightened and far-sighted to include the employment of talented Hindus in the senior administrative posts of a regime hitherto, in theory at least, conceived as exclusively Muslim.

But all that was still in the future and the first years of the reign were far from savoury. The ruler was young and hitherto his life had been spent in the shadow of the harem where a former wet-nurse, Maham Anka, exercised a powerful influence over him in the interests of her son, Adham Khan. The day-to-day administration was concentrated in the able hands of a Turkoman *amir* of Humayun's, Bayram Khan, who had long served the Mughul cause with devotion and had been the actual commander at the second battle of Panipat. But it was a relatively simple matter, as Akbar grew older, for his entourage to instil into the boy's head mistrust of his all-powerful minister. After a regency of four years the inevitable rupture occurred: Bayram Khan was dismissed from court, set out for Mecca, changed his mind and returned without permission, set out again and was finally murdered in Gujarat by a man with whom he had a blood-feud. Akbar's personal responsibility for these events remains uncertain but he took charge of Bayram Khan's son, Abd al-Rahim Khan, who was eventually granted his father's title of Khan-i Khanan and who was appointed to fill some of the highest offices of state, including the guardianship of the heir to the throne. One of the most distinguished figures of Akbar's court, renowned as a scholar and as the translator of Babur's memoirs from Chaghatai Turkish into Persian (his father had been a poet in both languages), his career is commemorated by a fine tomb with a superbly proportioned 'Tatar' dome in the southern part of Nizamuddin which must be rated among the most impressive of Delhi's lesser-known monuments.

Bayram Khan's death in 1560 was followed by a predictable increase in petticoat government as Maham Anka strengthened her hold over the young ruler. Her son, however, overplayed his hand and during the Mughul conquest of Malwa his failure to hand over to Akbar the booty of Mandu until compelled to do so showed a dangerous spirit of insubordination. His arrogance finally led him to stab the *vakil*, Ataga Khan, the husband of another of Akbar's wet-nurses, during a public audience given by the *vakil* and the infuriated emperor is said to have hurled the

19 Miniature: Akbar on an elephant pursuing another elephant across a bridge of boats which is collapsing. Outline by Basawan and painting by Chatai, late 16th century. *Akbarnameh. Victoria and Albert Museum, London*, I.S.2-1896 21/117. (35.4 × 22.2 cm.)

20 Miniature: Babur superintending the construction of the Bagh-i Vafa at Kabul. Painting by Bishandas and Nanha, c. 1590. *Baburnameh. Victoria and Albert Museum, London*. (22.5 × 15 cm.)

21 Miniature: Akbar directing the siege of the Rajput fortress of Ranthambhor, 1568. Painting by Muskin and Para (?). *Akbarnameh. Victoria and Albert Museum, London*, I.S.2-1896 72/117. (34.2 × 19.6 cm.)

22 Miniature: Akbar inspecting the building of Fatehpur Sikri. Outline by Tulsi the Elder, painting by Bandi and portraits by Mahhu the Younger. *Akbarnameh. Victoria and Albert Museum, London*, I.S.2-1896 91/117. (33.6 × 20.6 cm.)

درختهای انار هم هست کرد و کرد و حوض تمام سه برکه زار

جای عن باغ همین است در وقت زرد شدن نارنجهای بسیار

murderer over a balustrade on to the pavement beneath and then had him carried up and thrown down again until he was dead. Ataga Khan, the murdered *vakil*, was buried in a small but exquisite tomb on the northern edge of the Nizamuddin district while Adham Khan enjoyed the distinction of burial in the last octagonal tomb to be built in Delhi, a massive structure between the Qutb-Minar and Mehrauli on the southern ramparts of Lal-Kot.

Shortly after this incident (1562) Maham Anka died, and not very long afterwards Akbar himself came near to death when an assassin posted on the roof of Khair al-Manzel Masjid, a *madraseh* built by Maham Anka close to the Purana Qala, shot an arrow at the emperor as he was riding back into Delhi and wounded him in the shoulder. Whether the attempt on his life was connected with the violent events described above or with the emperor's current pursuit of certain women belonging to respected Delhi families, the fact remains that from about this time Akbar drew into his own hands the supervision of the whole administration of the empire and it was never again to be relegated to the charge of favourites or kinsmen. Not until 1564 did Akbar come completely into his own.

In any account of Akbar's reign war and rebellion must inevitably occupy the front of the stage. Aggression against one's weaker neighbours was an accepted maxim of the age and Akbar showed himself no different from his contemporaries when he declared:

'A sovereign should be ever intent on conquests, otherwise his neighbours will rise in arms against him. The army should be exercised in warfare, lest for want of training they become self-indulgent.'[7]

His natural ambition however, especially as a young man, must have been greatly stimulated both by the nobility, to whom warfare could be immensely profitable, and by the steady accumulation from year to year of ever-increasing numbers of soldiers, horses, elephants and guns; by the late sixteenth century a Mughul army in the field already resembled a city on the move (a century later it would be even more ponderous and exposed to attack, as the Marathas quickly discovered). Not all Akbar's military expeditions were expansionist, however, for he was also forced to quell formidable uprisings among his own followers, especially the Uzbeks settled in India who retained links with the Shaybanid courts beyond the Amu-Darya. Even more dangerous were the Afghans, many of whom had been born in the time of the Lodi Sultans and could still recall the great days of Sher Shah and his son when an Afghan sat upon the throne of Delhi. The Afghans in India – unlike the Central Asian Turks or the Indian Muslims – retained in their new home clan loyalties which made them, formidable fighters as they were, the most turbulent and dangerous of the emperor's subjects.

Yet foreign conquests there were, and on a remarkable scale. Malwa, Gondwana and Bengal were added to the empire and Mughul troops made their first appearance in the Deccan where, by the end of the reign, Khandesh, Berar and Ahmadnagar had become Mughul *subahs* (provinces). Savage campaigns were also waged against the Rajput princes but the most valuable prize of all came with the annexation of the formerly independent Sultanate of Gujarat which provided the empire with an enormous additional revenue from its rich commercial centres, access to the Gulf of Cambay, and hence to the Holy Cities of Arabia, and opportunities for trade with both the Portuguese and the Ottoman Empire.

Almost continuous warfare throughout the reign did not, however, prevent Akbar from devoting much of his time and energy to consolidating what he had already won and establishing a durable administrative system based upon founda-

23 Miniature: Akbar at the shrine of Khwaja Muin al-Din Chishti at Ajmer. Outside the shrine gifts are being distributed to the inhabitants of the city. Outline by Basawan, painting by Ikhlas, and portraits by Nanha. *Akbarnameh. Victoria and Albert Museum, London*, I.S.2-1896 23/117. (34.2 × 21.4 cm.)

24 Miniature: Akbar hunting blackbuck with cheetahs in the vicinity of Agra. Outline by Basawan and painting by Dharm Das. *Akbarnameh. Victoria and Albert Museum, London*, I.S.2-1896 24/117. (33.7 × 20.7 cm.)

25 Miniature: Akbar, lost while hunting wild asses near Multan in 1571, is discovered in an exhausted condition by his retinue. Outline and painting by Mashesh and portraits by Kisu. *Akbarnameh. Victoria and Albert Museum, London*, I.S.2-1896 84/117. (34.2 × 21.4 cm.)

26 The tomb of Humayun, Delhi. Rooftop view.

27 Jahangiri Mahal, Agra Fort. One of the few remaining buildings inside the fort dating from Akbar's reign, the interior of this palace was inspired by the example of the Man Mandir in Gwalior.

tions laid in the time of Sher Shah. In Raja Todar Mal he found the perfect executive officer to place the assessment and collection of the land revenue on a stable footing and much of Todar Mal's work was to survive the dissolution of the empire itself and in some areas provide the basis for the British revenue system of the early nineteenth century. From time to time Akbar also remitted unproductive or especially unpopular taxes, including taxes levied on Hindu pilgrims and the *jizya*, a poll-tax imposed by medieval Muslim rulers on *dhimmis* (non-Muslims) in return for granting them protected status. Akbar was not the only Indian Muslim ruler to take this step, and it is possible to exaggerate its significance, but the move was indicative of Akbar's bold and imaginative approach to the problems of his heterogeneous empire and may have reduced some of the permanent, although generally passive, Hindu antagonism towards an administration which was wholly Muslim in spirit. Probably of more significance at a purely political level was his policy of drawing the great Rajput chiefs into active partnership in the government of the empire (perhaps as a counter-weight to the untrustworthy Afghan element) by granting them posts of responsibility and honour in the imperial hierarchy. Eventually it became accepted practice for the ruler of, say, Amber or Jodhpur to be appointed governor of a major province, or commander-in-chief of an army composed largely of Muslims, while Rajput princesses were accorded royal rank in the imperial harem, where they were permitted to practise their own religion without molestation.

Akbar's policy towards his Hindu subjects must, however, be seen in proper perspective. Notwithstanding the opinions expressed in the writings and sermons of the *ulama*, the upholders of Muslim orthodoxy, the fact remains that under the pre-Mughul Sultans of Delhi (and even more under the Mughuls) there were important areas of social life where Muslim and Hindu did have frequent contact with each other; not only Muslim sovereigns but also the entire Muslim ruling class employed Hindus in their service, often in positions of the greatest responsibility (as was the case with Todar Mal and his staff) as well as in humbler capacities – as craftsmen, artisans, entertainers, concubines, soldiers and servants. Thus the two communities were unable to ignore each other's existence – at least in the great cities of the north – and wherever they mingled in close proximity, whether at court or in camp, in the celebration of time-honoured festivals or in the intimacy of the harem, differences could be forgotten and distinctions blurred. Nor is it too fanciful to suppose that when the Turkish and Persian conquerors of northern India, despite their pride of race and religion, succumbed to the compelling beauty of Indian women this would have been the first and perhaps the most irrevocable step towards their Indianization. Much of the Muslim architecture of the fifteenth and sixteenth centuries embodied this process of cross-fertilization. So did popular religious movements. In cities like Delhi and Ajmer the cells of Chishti saints, often located in the poorest and most thickly-populated parts of the town, had long served as common ground where members of the two communities might meet, but in the early Mughul period the popularity of Sufism among Muslims, and the emergence of the Bhakti movement within the folds of Hinduism, contributed to that mood of cultural synthesis and religious syncretism which characterizes both the reign of Akbar and his own highly complex personality.

Born at Amarkot in Sind in 1542, Akbar's childhood was spent in present-day Afghanistan and he was twelve when he re-entered India with his father's conquering army. Not a drop of Indian blood flowed in his veins. From his Persian mother he inherited his princely manners, his love of literature and the arts, and a characteristically Persian delight in philosophical discussion. From his Turkish father came his fierce energy, his love of war and his ability to command, and when he later learnt to absorb so much of what was genuinely Indian, and therefore alien to his upbringing, he was only displaying to the full the Turkish genius for assimilating the essence of alien civilizations. His Chingizkhanid ancestry was another strand to be reckoned with, giving him a charismatic authority over his Mughul followers and perhaps stimulating his ambition to found a great empire for himself in the manner of his Mongol forebears whose exploits were illustrated by his court-painters. Like them, too, he delighted in accounts of faraway places and strange customs while the friendly protection which he extended to Brahmins, Jains, Christian missionaries and Parsees is reminiscent of the way in which the sons and grandsons of Chingiz Khan welcomed Buddhist lamas, Taoist hermits and Nestorian priests to their encampments.

The Mongols had revelled in warfare, oblivious of human suffering or loss of life, and during his early years at least Akbar showed himself little different from his ancestors. Accounts of the reign contain descriptions of prisoners being blinded, maimed and executed by being trampled under the feet of elephants. The massacre of opponents or prisoners was not unusual and at the siege of Chitor (1568) the frightful Rajput rite of *jauhar* was followed – upon the Mughul capture of the fort – by Akbar's command that all the survivors should be killed. After a battle outside Ahmadabad in 1573 he ordered a pyramid of skulls to be constructed from the heads of the rebel soldiers.

All this serves to emphasize the fact that during Akbar's lifetime the Mughuls who had settled in India had still not broken free from their Central Asian heritage. Many among the older generation continued to retain family ties north of the Hindu Kush and Chaghatai Turkish, although declining in importance with each succeeding generation, survived side by side with Persian as the language of the Mughul court down to the early eighteenth century, spoken and read, for example, by all Aurangzeb's sons. It was probably not until after the close of the sixteenth century that the Mughuls ceased to feel themselves strangers in a strange land. To the new generation the pastures of the Amu-Darya and the fabled cities of Mawarannahr meant only the land where its ancestors had lived in splendour. Yet for many years to come the imagery of Iran and Central Asia would provide the inspiration for Mughul poets, who sang of the heroes and heroines of Firdowsi and Nizami in gardens peopled with the inventions of Persian mythology and stocked with Persian birds and flowers. For such as these neither the Indian countryside nor its folklore had any real meaning.

Among the Chingizkhanid traditions to survive in Mughul India none was more spectacular than the employment of the troops, when not actually on campaign, in great *battues* in which the soldiers fanned out over many miles of country and day by day, often for weeks on end, slowly drove the game into a steadily contracting circle in which first the ruler and his family, then his *amirs* and subordinate commanders, and finally the soldiers themselves slaughtered every remaining living creature. The object of this butchery was not solely to procure the meat, hide and furs from the animals but also to keep the army fit, to practise disciplined movements over a large area and to improve each man's horsemanship and archery. During the early part of his life Akbar took the greatest delight in these massacres and in 1567, for example, it is recorded that he held one near Lahore in which an area of forty square miles around the city was beaten and altogether some 15,000 deer, nilghai, foxes and jackals were slaughtered. A keen *shikari* himself, Akbar revelled in all the varied pleasures of the chase, from facing charging tigers and leopards to pursuing the wild ass in the Rajasthan desert after the manner of the ancient kings of Iran (cf. pls. 24, 25). Another of his favourite occupations was elephant-fighting and on at least one occasion he insisted on mounting one of the infuriated beasts – with almost fatal results. Courage of this sort, whether displayed on the battlefield or on a hunting excursion, goes a long way towards explaining the intense admiration and devotion which he was able to arouse among his followers.

During the early part of his reign Akbar's attitude towards Islam was not noticeably unorthodox and the *ulama* were accorded appropriate respect as the pillars of an essentially Muslim state. He reserved his personal veneration, however, for the *shaykhs* and *pirs* of the dervish-orders (*silsila*) which were as characteristic of Indian as of Central Asian Islam. He visited the shrine of Khwaja Muin al-Din Chishti (cf. pl. 23) at Ajmer annually and at the siege of Chitor vowed that, if successful, he would make the pilgrimage to Ajmer on foot. The foundation of a new capital at Fatehpur Sikri originated with a similar vow when a celebrated Chishti saint, Shaykh Salim, whose hermit's cell was situated at Sikri, some twenty-six miles west of Agra, prophesied the birth of an heir to the throne. When next one of Akbar's wives became pregnant (a Rajput princess from Amber) she was sent to the Shaykh's cell for her confinement. The child born there (the future Emperor Jahangir) was given the name of Salim in honour of the Shaykh. A second son, Murad, was also born there while a third son, Daniyal, was born in the house of another celebrated saint, Shaykh Daniyal, at Ajmer. In such matters Akbar possessed to the full the conventional piety of the age and in some respects he went further than some other Muslim rulers of India, although he was always very tolerant towards non-Muslims. Following his conquest of Gujarat, for example, he established an annual expedition to Mecca, led by one of the greatest nobles of the court, and in this way ensured that pilgrims from India – and even from Mawarannahr and Khurasan – could make the *hajj* with the maximum security.

As he grew older, however, Akbar became increasingly critical of the conventional Muslim outlook of his times and bitterly antagonistic to the claims of the *ulama* to speak for the whole Muslim community in matters of belief. This changing attitude of Akbar was undoubtedly connected with the growth of his comprehensive vision of an empire embracing diversity of faith and culture – but it was also a reflection of the hardening of his iron-willed, fiercely individualistic personality. His interest in non-Muslim culture and the favour with which he treated his non-Muslim subjects infuriated the *ulama* and their hostility to his behaviour only stimulated all the more his determination to do as he pleased. The culmination of years of antagonism between the emperor and his orthodox opponents came with his establishment of the *Din-i Ilahi* ('Divine Faith'), a new syncretistic religion which does not seem to have extended beyond a small circle of intimate companions and which withered away during the last years of the reign, largely through indifference. It is impossible to gauge what Akbar intended by this confrontation with the Muslim Establishment. It may have sprung from some genuine spiritual illumination or it may have consisted largely of a piece of private make-believe among a clique of courtiers. Perhaps the most charitable explanation of the *Din-i Ilahi* is to interpret it as an Augustan dream of uniting the diverse elements of a highly cosmopolitan empire by means of an imperial rite centred on the person of the *padshah* (emperor).

It would be a superficial reading of the situation, however, to see Akbar as an isolated protagonist on behalf of religious and cultural synthesis; in the poetry of the period, for example, there is evidence to suggest that such an attitude was by no means as rare as has sometimes been supposed. Another aspect of the cosmo-

28 Fatehpur Sikri. Detail of the sandstone carving in the so-called Turkish Sultana's Palace.

29 Jami Masjid, Fatehpur Sikri. Marble screen in the tomb of Shaykh Salim Chishti.

30 Fatehpur Sikri. Detail of the sandstone carving in the house of Raja Birbal, a Brahmin from Orchha and one of Akbar's most intimate associates.

31 Jami Masjid, Fatehpur Sikri. The porch of the tomb of Shaykh Salim Chishti. The foundations of this tomb were laid in 1571, the year of the saint's death.

31

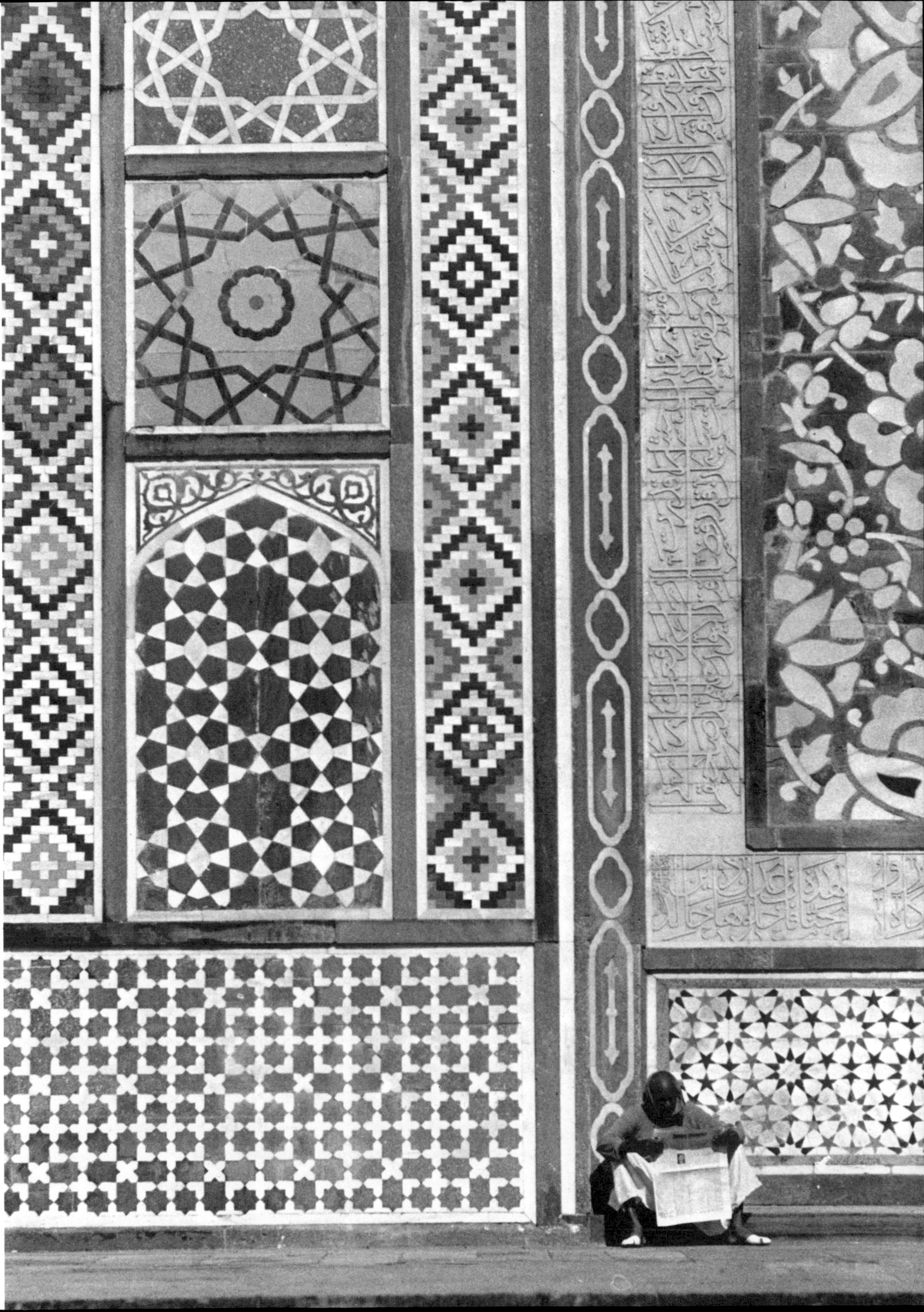

35

politan spirit of the reign was the encouragement given to translations of all kinds. While a number of Persian classics were rendered into Sanskrit and Hindi, the greater part of this activity took the form of translations of religious literature into Persian from other languages – Chaghatai Turkish, Kashmiri, Sanskrit, Arabic, etc. In this way Akbar's school of translators made a valuable contribution to the Indianization of the Mughul ruling class.

The other aspects of the literary culture of Akbar's court, on the other hand, only served to emphasize its foreign – and primarily Persian – origin. The historians of the reign consciously wrote in a Persian historiographical tradition, the ornate rhetoric of Abul Fazl drawing its inspiration from Il-Khanid models while the more prosaic narratives of Nizam al-Din Ahmad and Abdul Qadir Badaoni recall older, pre-Mongol traditions of Persian prose-composition. Badaoni, a scholarly representative of the *ulama* class and enough of a Sanskritist to render the *Ramayana* into Persian and to take part in the joint-translation of the *Mahabharata*, was the waspish Saint-Simon of the court, hating Akbar for his heterodoxy yet compelled to recognize his greatness even while abusing him in secret. In poetry the period was characterized not only by prolific output but also by writing of real merit and the familiar cliché about the reign of Akbar being the Indian summer of Persian poetry is not far from the mark. Naziri, Faizi and Urfi would have ranked as major figures in any age and in India they are reckoned among the finest of poets (Iqbal at one period of his life rated Urfi even above Hafiz), although rather less highly esteemed in Iran, the land of their birth. The Persian origin of most of the greatest literary figures of the period is an inescapable fact. When, for example, Abul Fazl lists the fifty-nine poets at Akbar's court whom he considered the most talented, he names the place of origin of forty-seven of them and only two come from the sub-continent itself (Kashmir). The remainder originate in the ancient centres of Persian civilization, far to the west and north-west, the majority coming from Shiraz, Isfahan, Kashan, Ray, Mashhad, Herat, Merv and Bukhara.

If Delhi and Agra in the sixteenth century were in so many ways cultural colonies of Iran, this trend owed a good deal to Akbar himself. In the preceding pages his Chingizkhanid blood and his Central Asian heritage have been stressed to explain at least part of his enigmatic personality and his career of conquest. But there is the other side of the medal – the bibliophile and collector of manuscripts who, although perhaps scarcely literate, loved to be read to and who combined a remarkably retentive memory with a keen intellectual appetite and well-developed critical faculties. This was part of his Persian heritage and Abul Fazl's list of Akbar's favourite books reveals the taste of a polished Persian gentleman: it includes the *Shahnameh*, Nizami's *Khamseh*, the *Masnavi* of Jalal al-Din Rumi, the *Diwan* of Hafiz, and the complete works of Jami. The list is not strikingly original but the emphasis on poetry and mysticism is unmistakable and Abul Fazl specifically states that it was Rumi and Hafiz who made the most powerful impression upon the emperor's mind.

The vigorous personal influence which Akbar exercised over the literary life of his court had its parallel in his patronage of painting and it was during his reign that the early Safavid style, introduced into India by Humayun, began to merge with indigenous Indian elements and a genuinely original Mughul style evolved, wholly emancipated from the influence of Herat, Bukhara or Tabriz. With the new style came a change of emphasis in subject-matter. Traditional Persian painting had been mainly (although not exclusively) concerned with the illustration of literary classics such as the *Shahnameh*, Nizami's *Khamseh* and Jami's *Yusuf va Zulaykha*. From Akbar's time onwards, however, Mughul painters – many of them

Hindus – while continuing to illustrate the great classics of Persian literature, turned increasingly to new subjects, such as the life of the ruler and his court, the representation of nature, landscape and portraiture. The most ambitious work to be undertaken in Akbar's *ateliers*, the series of illustrations commissioned for Abul Fazl's *Akbarnameh*, demonstrate the distinctive qualities of the nascent Mughul School which sets it so far apart from its Safavid or Timurid precursors – its crowded, bustling scenes of men and animals, full of vigour and movement; its uninhibited use of colour; its observation of detail; and its rejection of the languid, elegant formalism of the late Herat or Bukhara Schools – giving a visual dimension to the history of the reign unequalled in any previous period of Muslim history (cf pls. 19, 21, 22, 23, 24, 25, 65).

Unlike Babur or Humayun, Akbar had both the time and the resources to build on a monumental scale although it was in or near Agra rather than Delhi that the most important Mughul buildings of the second half of the sixteenth century were constructed. Akbar appears to have had no great affection for Delhi and his reasons can well be imagined. Although far larger and more splendid than Agra at the time of his accession, Delhi must have been for him a city of unpleasant memories, the scene of his father's death, his own narrowly-escaped assassination and the disreputable events of his early years on the throne. Moreover its principal landmarks – the Purana Qala, and the city walls and gateways – commemorated the greatness of Sher Shah, whom he regarded as the usurper of his father's kingdom. Of more practical importance, as the capital of both the Lodi and Sur dynasties, Delhi must have contained a considerable Afghan element, always restless and basically hostile to the Mughuls. Under these circumstances Agra, where associations with Afghan rule were less strong, must have seemed a more attractive residence. Not that Akbar avoided Delhi. Accounts of the reign record regular visits by the court and on these occasions, at least in his early years when he was still relatively orthodox, the emperor used to visit not only his father's newly-completed mausoleum beside the Jumna but also the tombs of celebrated *shaykhs* and *sayyids* in its vicinity. He likewise hunted over much of the area now covered by the residential colonies of New Delhi as well as in the countryside around Mehrauli and Palam.

Akbar's greatest undertaking in Agra was the construction of an immensely strong fortress beside the Jumna to replace the decaying brick-built citadel of Sultan Iskandar Lodi. Unfortunately, apart from the gateways, the outer walls and the moat, little survives of Akbar's original structure. When his grandson, Shah Jahan, decided to reconstruct the interior of the fort he demolished practically every building dating from Akbar's time except the Jahangiri Mahal (cf. pl. 27), a palace built in the Hindu tradition by Hindu architects and craftsmen recruited from Rajasthan or, more probably, from the Gwalior region. There is a strong presumption that the Jahangiri Mahal is partly modelled on the Man Mandir, the palace of Maharaja Man Singh (1486–1516) at Gwalior, which was later to become one of the principal Mughul state prisons. It is fortunate, however, that there has been preserved virtually intact at Fatehpur Sikri the complete physical environment in which Akbar, his family and his courtiers lived. Both as evidence for the domestic arrangements of Akbar's household and as an unsurpassed essay in the combination of Muslim and Hindu styles, Fatehpur Sikri must rank among the most important surviving Mughul monuments. In the history of the dynasty itself, however, this *folie de grandeur* enjoyed only a brief moment of glory. The site, chosen primarily because it had been the residence of Shaykh Salim, proved unhealthy and there were frequent shortages of water. Most of the buildings were

Fig. 9 Drawing of Akbar as an old man, probably done towards the close of the 16th century. *Johnson 57. 1, India Office Library, London.*

36 Buland Darwaza of the Jami Masjid, seen from a lane in Fatehpur Sikri.

37 Jami Masjid, Fatehpur Sikri. Detail of the cedarwood and mother-of-pearl canopy over the tomb of Shaykh Salim Chishti.

38 The so-called Turkish Sultana's Palace, Fatehpur Sikri. This residence was built either for Akbar's first wife, Ruqayeh Begum, or for Salimeh Sultana Begum, a former wife of Bayram Khan before she was married to Akbar. Both women were nieces of Humayun.

39 Akbar's tomb, Sikandra. The entrance gateway looking towards the mausoleum.

40 Akbar's tomb, Sikandra, from the entrance gateway.

41 Akbar's tomb, Sikandra. Tilework on the facade.

37

38

40

41

44

45

constructed between 1569 and 1585 but thereafter Akbar seems to have lost interest in the project and, although it was still inhabitated during the reign of Jahangir, its long decline had already begun.

Here Akbar encouraged a synthesis of Muslim and Hindu artistic traditions to a far greater extent than in the later Persianized buildings of the time of Shah Jahan. His architects had inherited from the Sur period a severe but by no means inelegant style of domestic and military architecture which was to be used to good effect in the construction of the forts at Allahabad, Agra, Ajmer, Lahore and Attock, while the design of mausoleums either followed Lodi prototypes (as in the case of the tomb of Adham Khan at Mehrauli) or the Persianized style of Humayun's tomb and the tomb of Ataga Khan in Nizamuddin. At Fatehpur Sikri, however, while the fortifications and entrance gateways are clearly derived from the Purana Qala, the main residential accommodation – especially the Jodh Bai palace (cf. pl. 18) and Birbal's house (cf. pl. 30) – has a distinctly Hindu character, reflecting both the non-communal composition of the court and the emperor's concept of a universal empire unfettered by Muslim particularist traditions. The only building at Fatehpur Sikri which can be said to be unambiguously Muslim in its architecture is, very properly, the Jami Masjid itself, built between 1571 and 1575.

The cultural synthesis achieved in the architecture of Fatehpur Sikri reached its culmination in Akbar's tomb at Sikandra, five miles beyond Agra on the Delhi road. This is a Muslim mausoleum which could not have been built anywhere but in India and where the architectural conception is wholly indigenous, notwithstanding the Persian setting of a walled garden with four tiled gateways (cf. pl. 35). It would be rash, however, to ascribe too much at Sikandra to the personal influence of Akbar himself; the structure was far from complete at the time of his death in 1605 and Jahangir relates in his memoirs how he frequently interfered with its construction, re-designing some features and changing others, while the highest storey clearly reflects the taste of Jahangir's reign. As it stands today, the entire complex owes perhaps almost as much to the son as to the father.

In the early nineteenth century Bishop Heber called Sikandra 'the most splendid building in its way which I had yet seen in India', and his description is still sufficiently vivid to be worth quoting in full.

'It stands in a square area of about forty English acres, enclosed by an embattled wall, with octagonal towers at the angles surmounted by open pavilions, and four very noble gateways of red granite, the principal of which is inlaid with white marble, and has four high marble minarets. The space within is planted with trees and divided into green alleys, leading to the central building, which is a sort of solid pyramid surrounded externally with cloisters, galleries, and domes, diminishing gradually on ascending it, till it ends in a square platform of white marble, surrounded by most elaborate lattice-work of the same material, in the centre of which is a small altar tomb, also of white marble, carved with a delicacy and beauty which do full justice to the material, and to the graceful forms of Arabic characters which form its chief ornament. At the bottom of the building, in a small but very lofty vault, is the real tomb of this great monarch, plain and unadorned, but also of white marble.'[8] (cf. pls. 39, 40, 41.)

Opinions may differ as to the effectiveness of the total ensemble but its association with India's only Muslim ruler whose memory is still widely respected by Hindus gives it a peculiar fascination, since it enshrines not only Akbar's earthly remains but also his ideal of a cultural synthesis among his subjects which gives him a unique place in Indian history.

Fig. 10 Gold *mohur* of Jahangir, with a portrait of Akbar, minted at Agra, A.H. 1014 (A.D. 1605–6). *British Museum, London.* (*Actual size*)

42 Itimad al-Dowleh's tomb, Agra. Itimad al-Dowleh was the father of Nur Jahan, who built his tomb in 1626, and the grandfather of Mumtaz Mahal.

43 Itimad al-Dowleh's tomb, Agra. Detail of the marble floor of the tomb-chamber.

44 Itimad al-Dowleh's tomb, Agra. Marble screen.

45 Itimad al-Dowleh's tomb, Agra. Detail of the *pietra dura* decoration.

46 Chini-ka-Rauza, Agra. Detail of the tomb of Alami Afzal Khan Shirazi, one of the most distinguished nobles of Shah Jahan's court. The tomb was built in 1639.

47 Miniature: Prince Salim (afterwards the Emperor Jahangir) as a young man. Painting by Bichitr, c. 1630, presumably copied from an earlier portrait after Jahangir's death. *Victoria and Albert Museum, London,* I.M.28-1925. (25 × 18.1 cm.)

1605–1657

Akbar laid the foundations of Mughul rule in India so firmly that for a further century after his death the frontiers of the empire continued to expand and it was only in the second quarter of the eighteenth century that undisguisable decrepitude set in. During his reign of fifty years so much wealth had been accumulated in the political and commercial centres of northern India that his two immediate successors, Jahangir and Shah Jahan, were able to surround themselves with a degree of splendour and opulence unequalled by any other Muslim dynasty. Fortunately both men, despite the obvious failings which accompany unlimited opportunities for self-indulgence, possessed in some degree qualities which fitted them for the role of presiding over the culminating half century of Mughul civilization between 1605 and 1657: they were alike in possessing excellent taste, a keen interest in the visual arts and unstinting generosity towards artists and men of letters.

Probably Jahangir and Shah Jahan, both of whom had Rajput mothers, felt themselves to be far more a part of India that Akbar could ever have done and the same must have been true of many of their courtiers. The first generation of Mughul poets in India had willingly commiserated with their masters on the hardships of life in their hot and dusty land of exile but Shah Jahan's poet-laureate, Abu Talib Kalim, a Persian born in Hamadan and reared in Kashan, mirrored the changing attitude of the Mughul *élite* when he wrote of India:

'One can say of it that it is a second Paradise in this respect,
That whoever leaves this garden is filled with regret.'[9]

The circumstances surrounding Jahangir's birth have been described in the previous chapter. This long-awaited heir passed from childhood to maturity adored but always over-shadowed by his father and, being a far weaker personality than Akbar, he grew up resentful of his masterful parent and bitterly jealous of Akbar's long-established coterie of advisers who must often have come between father and son. For Abul Fazl, in particular, he felt an almost pathological hatred which reached its climax in the scholar's assassination in 1602. From then until Akbar's death three years later Jahangir remained in a state of semi-revolt, the two only becoming reconciled at Akbar's death-bed in Agra.

As in the case of his father but unlike his own son and grandson, Jahangir – now turned thirty-six – ascended the throne unaccompanied by any family bloodletting; both his younger brothers had already drunk themselves to death during the previous reign. Despite an acute intelligence, Jahangir was generally indifferent to the larger interests of the empire. He lacked any obvious inclination for warfare and was bored by the humdrum details of day-to-day administration. Self-indulgent and sensual, a compulsive drinker with a pronounced streak of cruelty emanating from a weak personality, his character and outlook recalled some of those less distinguished Timurid ancestors from beyond the Hindu Kush among

48 Miniature: Shah Jahan enthroned. Painting by Nadir az-Zaman, 1627–57. *Gift of Alexander Smith Cochran, 1913, Metropolitan Museum of Art, New York.* (35.5 × 24 cm.)

49 Miniature: Lovers on a terrace. Painting by Govardhan, c. 1630. *Collection of Alice and Nasli Heeramaneck, New York.* (15.5 × 12 cm.)

50 Miniature: Prince Parviz, younger brother of Prince Khurram (afterwards the Emperor Shah Jahan), with female attendants on a terrace. Painting by Govardhan. *Chester Beatty Library, Dublin*, Ms. 7 fo. 2. (22.2 × 13.4 cm.)

51 Miniature: Raja Jaswant Singh of Marwar (Jodhpur), one of the principal Rajput feudatories of the empire during the reigns of Shah Jahan and Aurangzeb, c. 1650. *British Museum, London.* (16.5 × 26.5 cm.)

52 Miniature: Jahangir embracing Nur Jahan while receiving a cup of wine from a female attendant. Painting by Govardhan (?), c. 1615. *Collection of Alice and Nasli Heeramaneck, New York.* (17.5 × 11.5 cm.)

53 Itimad al-Dowleh's tomb, Agra.

بماند سالها این نظم ترتیب
که هستی را نمی بینم بقایی
غرض نقشیست کز ما یاد ماند
ز ما هر ذره خاک افتد بجایی
مگر صاحبدلی روزی برحمت
کند در حق درویشان دعائی

49

50

51

52

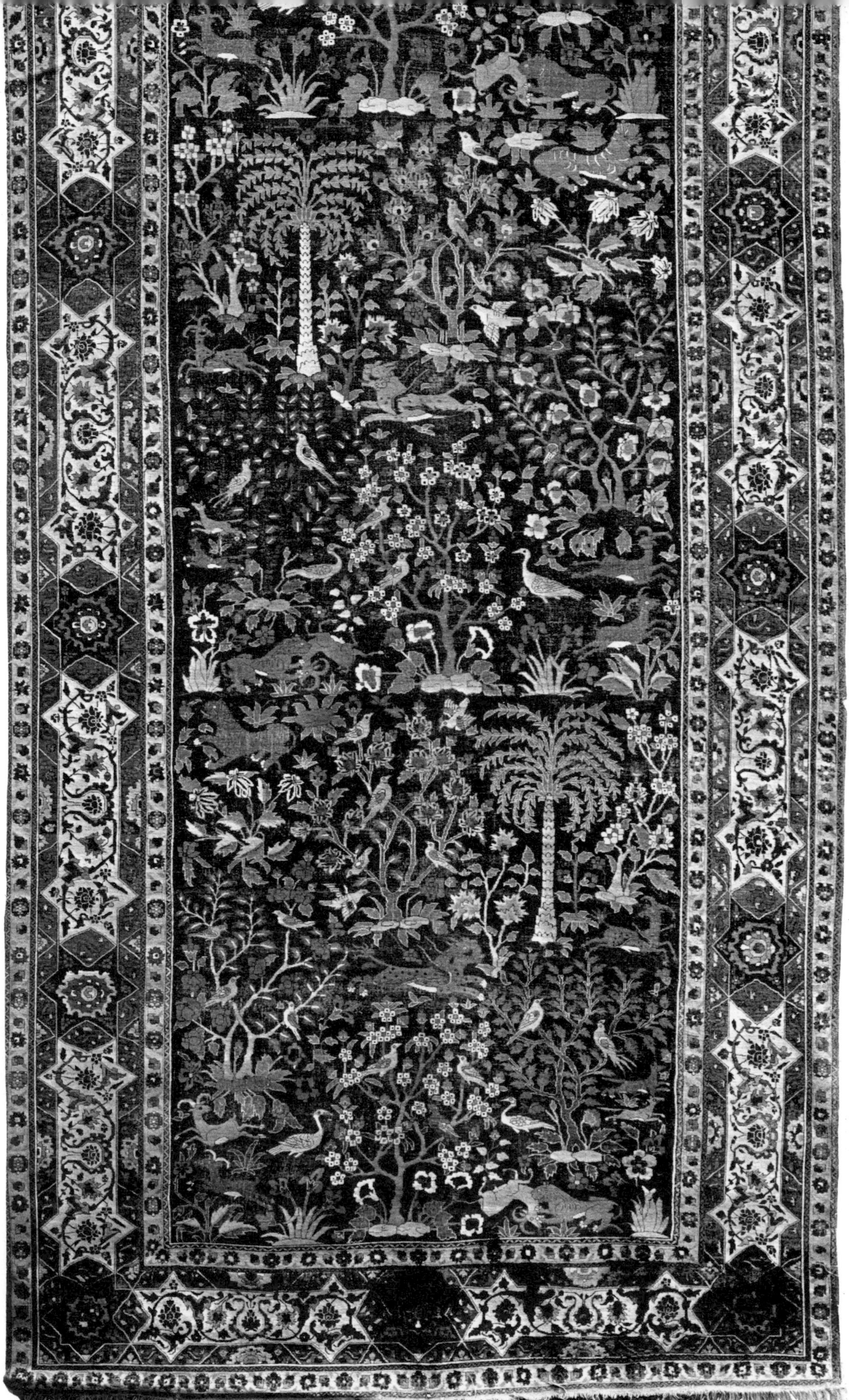

whom Babur had spent his early years; as ruler of Farghana or Badakhshan he would probably have earned a footnote in history as a patron and connoisseur. As the master of a great empire he was utterly undistinguished, and the fact that the twenty-two years of his reign saw no visible weakening in the fabric of Mughul government is a measure of the solidity of Akbar's achievement and also a tribute to the good sense of the Mughul ruling class which appreciated that the maintenance of stability was in its own interests. Thus even with Jahangir's loose grasp of the reins the imperial frontiers continued to move forward – in Bengal, in Mewar and in Ahmadnagar – and the only major reverse was in 1622 when Shah Abbas, the Safavid ruler of Iran, seized Kandahar with impunity.

Despite his Rajput mother, Jahangir seems to have disliked the Indian plains; he preferred Lahore to Delhi or Agra but it was Kashmir which he loved best and it was during his reign that regular journeys across the Pir Panjal became an established feature of court life. In Kashmir he could escape the ceaseless round of business and public appearances which enveloped him in the cities of the plains and enter an idyllic private world where, like Louis XV in the gardens of the Trianon, he could indulge his love of nature and feminine company undisturbed. Throughout his life he lived under the spell of personalities more colourful than his own and of these the most influential was to be the beautiful Nur Jahan, whom he married in 1611 when she was already thirty-four and who, for the remainder of the reign, would be the real ruler of the empire (cf. pl. 52).

Nur Jahan's Persian grandfather had been in the service of Shah Tahmasb and had died in Yazd laden with honours. His heirs, however, soon fell upon evil days so that his son, Mirza Ghiyas al-Din Muhammad, was forced to set out for India with his family. It was on this journey, at Kandahar in 1577, that his wife gave birth to a daughter, Mihr al-Nisa, to whom Jahangir would one day give the name of Nur Mahal ('Light of the Palace') and then Nur Jahan ('Light of the World'). Mirza Ghiyas al-Din Muhammad made his way to Akbar's court at Fatehpur Sikri where, being an able man, he rose rapidly in the imperial hierarchy, holding a number of important posts including that of *diwan* of Kabul and ending his days with the rank of a commander of 7,000 and the proud title of Itimad al-Dowleh ('Pillar of the State'). One of the band of Persian exiles whose polished manners and polite learning added so much brilliance to Akbar's court, he was excelled in almost every respect by his son, Asaf Khan, an urbane and affable courtier and an outstanding fiscal administrator who, secure in the favour of both Jahangir and Shah Jahan, attained the highest provincial governorships and finally the rank of commander-in-chief. In 1612, a year after his sister's marriage to Jahangir, Asaf Khan arranged for his daughter, Arjumand Banu Begum, to marry Prince Khurram, one of the emperor's younger sons. Fifteen years later Khurram was to ascend the throne as the Emperor Shah Jahan and Arjumand Banu Begum, Nur Jahan's niece, was to win immortality as Mumtaz Mahal, the woman in whose honour the Taj Mahal was to be built.

Such was the family which now ruled the empire in Jahangir's name but, talented though they were, Nur Jahan excelled them all in every way. An excellent conversationalist, a poet herself and a fine judge of Persian poetry, her accomplishments made her an irresistible companion and her taste extended beyond the patronage of painting and architecture to the decoration of rooms and the designing of ornaments, brocades, carpets and dresses so that the fashions in women's clothing adopted in her time were still in vogue at the end of the century. Jahangir was devoted to her and probably part of her attraction lay in her willingness to share his interests as a patron and collector and to assist him in the

Fig. 11   Gold *mohur* of Jahangir, with a portrait of the emperor holding a wine-cup. No mint stated. A.H. 1020 (A.D. 1611–2). *British Museum, London.* (*Actual size*).

54   Itimad al-Dowleh's tomb, Agra. Detail of the *pietra dura* decoration.

55   Miniature: Jahangir watching an elephant-fight. *Rogers Fund, 1912, Metropolitan Museum of Art, New York.* (44.5 × 30.5 cm.)

56   Part of a Mughul carpet dating from the reign of Jahangir (1605–27). The complete carpet is 8.22 × 2.75 m. *Gift of J. Pierpont Morgan, 1917, Metropolitan Museum of Art, New York.*

57   Taj Mahal, Agra. Moonlight view.

laying-out of Persian gardens, such as the beautiful Shalimar-Bagh on the Dal Lake in Kashmir. Jahangir's love of flowers and animals is reflected in the numerous miniatures painted at his behest by artists who shared their master's keen eye for the beauties of nature and there can be no doubt that he took a very personal interest in the work done in his *ateliers*. Sir Thomas Roe, the ambassador of James I of England, was amazed at his knowledge and discriminating taste where pictures were concerned.

In contrast to his preoccupation with painting, Jahangir seems to have taken relatively little interest in architecture but there is one building dating from his reign which ranks among the finest achievements of the Mughul spirit. This is the tomb built at Agra by Nur Jahan for her father, Itimad al-Dowleh, in a garden across the river from the city. It is constructed of the finest white marble inlaid with semi-precious stones (cf. pls. 42, 43, 53). Like the Taj Mahal itself, of which it is an immediate precursor and which, on a diminutive scale, it rivals for delicacy and lightness, the tomb of Itimad al-Dowleh (together with the almost contemporary tomb of the Khan-i Khanan in Delhi) marks the re-appearance in Mughul architecture of that Safavid element – to a great extent submerged at Fatehpur Sikri and Sikandra – which was to impose itself upon so much of the work done in Agra and Delhi in the second quarter of the seventeenth century.

His successor was his second son, Prince Khurram, who ascended the throne as Shah Jahan ('King of the World') in 1627 and who reigned until 1657 when he was deposed by his own son. Historians have tended to underestimate Shah Jahan, writing him off as a gross debauchee redeemed only by his depth of feeling for his dead queen which would express itself in the construction of the world's most beautiful mausoleum. In fact, he was an exceedingly able man – less of a statesman than Akbar and less conscientious than Aurangzeb – but still in the first rank of Indian rulers and one who, unlike Jahangir, recognized that kingship was a serious business. Endowed with all the qualities required of a medieval Muslim ruler, a brave and competent commander and a generous master who knew well how to combine dignity with affability when dealing with his servants, Shah Jahan prided himself on his strict sense of justice and the personal interest which he took in supervising the administrative machinery of the empire. The vices which the twentieth century condemns – his ruthlessness towards rival members of his own family, his extravagance, self-indulgence and promiscuity – must have seemed far less reprehensible in a seventeenth-century setting. It was Aurangzeb, however, who was to point out the fundamental flaw in his father's character: an indolence of spirit which impelled him to delegate excessive authority to his children and the principal *amirs* so that, as the years passed, he grew steadily out of touch with the day-to-day problems of imperial government. Yet, notwithstanding this and other defects, he set an indelible stamp upon his age; Delhi and Agra are as intimately associated with his name as is Isfahan with that of Shah Abbas or St Petersburg with that of Catherine the Great.

Shah Jahan was already a mature thirty-five when he succeeded his father in 1627 and from the outset he enjoyed the support of experienced administrators from the previous reign, such as his father-in-law, Asaf Khan, and an old enemy of Nur Jahan, Mahabat Khan, whose loyalty preserved the throne for him during the fratricidal struggle which followed close upon the announcement of Jahangir's death. In contrast, therefore, with the opening of the previous reign, Shah Jahan's administration was seasoned and sure of itself from the beginning, while for the next three decades continuity was maintained by able men in no way inferior to the best of Akbar's servants, such as the celebrated *vakil*, Saadullah Khan.

Fig. 12 Agate medallion representing Jahangir killing a lion. *Bibliothèque Nationale, Paris.*

58 Taj Mahal, Agra. Dawn view from the Jumna.

59 Taj Mahal, Agra. Early morning.

60 Taj Mahal, Agra. Early-morning view of the entrance gateway.

61 Miniature: Shah Jahan in his fortieth year. Painting by Bichitr, c. 1631. *Victoria and Albert Museum, London,* I.M.17-1925. (26.1 × 17.5 cm.)

Shah Jahan revived Akbar's policy of pressing southwards against the independent Muslim Sultanates of the Deccan. Ahmadnagar was the first to collapse and its annexation was followed by strenuous attacks on Bijapur and Golconda. To offset these triumphs came humiliating reverses in the north and west. Determined to re-conquer ancestral possessions in Central Asia, Shah Jahan made more than one attempt to seize the ancient city of Balkh situated between the Hindu Kush and the Amu-Darya. Balkh itself fell in 1646 but shortage of supplies, the poor morale of the Mughul troops who after long residence in India no longer possessed the stamina for Central Asian warfare, and the encircling Uzbek forces drawn from as far away as Bukhara compelled Aurangzeb, as commander of the occupying army, to abandon the hard-won prize. Equally ineffectually Shah Jahan squandered vast sums in attempting the re-conquest of Kandahar against the forces of Shah Abbas II. The drain of revenue on these two frontier expeditions and on the campaigns in the Deccan was an appreciable factor in the approaching financial crisis of the empire, as was the expenditure incurred as a result of Shah Jahan's insatiable appetite for building on a grandiose scale.

During the early years of his reign Shah Jahan seems to have preferred Agra to Delhi as a place of residence and no doubt his preference was partly due to his preoccupation with the construction of the Taj Mahal and his other ambitious building schemes in its vicinity. Mumtaz Mahal had died in childbirth at Burhanpur in 1631 but her body had been brought to Agra for burial and work on her tomb must have begun shortly afterwards. According to the French jeweller, Tavernier, who claimed to have seen it begun and finished, the completion of the whole complex of buildings gave employment to twenty thousand workmen for twenty-two years at a time when the resources of the Mughul Empire were such that only the finest materials were utilized for its embellishment and when the quality of the craftsmanship available in northern India was probably superior to that of any previous period.

The Taj Mahal, which in style is in direct line of descent from the tombs of Humayun and the Khan-i Khanan in Delhi, stands on a white marble platform 22 feet high and 313 feet square at the far end of a large formal garden enclosed on three sides by lofty walls and gateways. On the fourth flows the river Jumna. Structurally, the Taj Mahal is built in the shape of a square with each of its four sides dominated by a deep recess 63 feet high but with its four corners bevelled to form what is, in fact, an octagon. Above this rises the graceful dome-drum capped by a 'Tatar' dome, modified to satisfy the taste of the period. The total height of the building – including the metal pinnacle surmounting the dome – is 243 feet (cf. pls. 58, 59, 60).

To the student of Islamic architecture the first and perhaps the most enduring impression left by this incomparable monument is its Persian origin. This is unmistakably architecture in the Safavid style – perhaps the greatest single achievement of Safavid art – and it is therefore ironical that it should so often be regarded as the quintessence of the Mughul spirit. The unique achievement of the Mughul style was its ability to produce a genuine synthesis of Hindu and Muslim elements – demonstrated in the secular buildings at Fatehpur Sikri and by Akbar's tomb at Sikandra – while few monuments in India are more obviously of Persian derivation than the Taj Mahal. In its solution to the problems of space and proportion, in the classical perfection of its shape, in its combination of monumentality and delicacy, and in the quality of its decoration it represents the culmination on Indian soil of the Persian genius at work. A leading art-historian, Hermann Goetz, has put all this another way when he writes:

'It [the Taj Mahal] is a work of the finest Safavid taste . . . Except for the use of the most immaculate Makrana marble which translates the gay and gaudy Persian taste into the dreamy, languid spirit of later Mughal art, there are in the Taj Mahal only a few other deviations from Safavid orthodoxy – the four Rajput *chhattrīs* around the dome, some differences in the proportion of the dome and dome drum (common, however, in the Deccan), and also the minarets, probably inspired by Mahmūd Khiljī's tomb at Māndū. It is one of the freaks of history that this "Wonder of the World", which is least characteristic of Mughal art, has become the classic representative and emblem of Mughal civilization.'[10]

Elsewhere Goetz has reiterated these views, maintaining that only with considerable qualification can the Taj Mahal be described as Indian.

'Its swivel dome on top of an octagonal structure of arched recesses and balconies, flanked by four minarets, on a terrace between a mosque and a hall for pilgrims and lying between the Jamna river and a geometrical garden, is of the purest Persian design, the creation of two Persian architects, Ustād Ahmad and Ustād Hamīd; and yet it is utterly un-Persian, thoroughly Indian in its spirit, chaste and pure, subdued and dreamy, the very antithesis to the gaudy vitality of genuine Persian works.'[11]

So familiar is the Taj Mahal from pictures and photographs that it is impossible that anyone today should approach it for the first time without already having a fairly clear preconception of what to expect. Yet of those who make the pilgrimage few come away disappointed and many more must share the reaction of a young recruit to the Indian Civil Service who recorded in his diary near the beginning of the present century: 'I could not look at it long: it made me feel the burden of my body – of the earth earthy'.[12] One notable exception was E. M. Forster who on his first visit thought it looked 'hideous and hard' but who, writing nine years later, admitted total conversion.

'. . . I have never seen the vision lovelier. I went up the left hand further minaret, and saw all the magnificent buildings glowing beneath me and all the country [it was September] steaming beneath a dim red and grey sky, and just as I thought nothing could be more beautiful a muezzin with a most glorious voice gave the evening call to prayer from a Mosque. "There is no God but God".'[13]

The construction of the Taj Mahal spanned the greater part of Shah Jahan's reign yet all that time the emperor was prodigiously busy with other large-scale building projects in both Agra and Delhi. In Agra itself the renovation of the interior of Akbar's great fort was a major undertaking, of which the Moti Masjid or Pearl Mosque (1646–53) (cf. pl. 112), the Diwan-i Khass or Hall of Private Audience and the adjoining apartments reserved for the use of the imperial family rank among the most exquisite achievements of the century. The builders of the sixteenth century had favoured a combination of red sandstone and pale cream marble but Shah Jahan's opulent taste preferred dazzling white marble, polished and inlaid with precious or semi-precious stones. It is this extensive use of white marble and *pietra dura* work (cf. pl. 54) rather than any pronounced Indian characteristics in the buildings of the period which distinguishes the Mughul style under Shah Jahan from the architecture of contemporary Isfahan.

Neither Akbar nor his son or grandson had seen any need to fortify Agra and, as a result, the city had expanded north and south from the fort along the west bank of the Jumna where twenty-five or thirty palaces belonging to the Mughul princes or the great *amirs* faced the river and afforded, according to the French traveller, Thévenot, writing in the reign of Aurangzeb,

Fig. 13 Gold *mohur* of Shah Jahan, minted at Shajahanabad, A.H. 1054 (A.D. 1644–5). *British Museum, London. (Actual size)*

66 Taj Mahal, Agra. Dawn view from the Jumna.

67 Taj Mahal, Agra. Minaret.

68 Taj Mahal, Agra. Facade.

69 Taj Mahal, Agra. View of the lower platform.

70

'... a most delightful prospect to those who are on the other side of the River, which would be a great deal more agreeable, were it not for the long Garden-walls, which contribute much to the rendering the Town so long as it is. There are upon the same line several less Palaces and other Buildings. All, being desirous to enjoy the lovely prospect and convenience of the Water of the Gemna [Jumna], endeavoured to purchase ground on that side, which is the cause that the town is very long but narrow, and excepting some fair Streets that are in it, all the rest are very narrow, and without Symmetry ...

The Town of Agra is Populous as a great Town ought to be, but not so as to be able to send out Two hundred thousand fighting men into the Field, as some have written. The Palaces and Gardens take up the greatest part of it, so that its extent is no infallible Argument of the number of its Inhabitants. The ordinary Houses are low, and those of the commoner sort of People are but Straw, containing but few People a piece; and the truth is, one may walk the Streets without being crouded, and meet with no throng but when the Court is there: But at that time, I have been told there is great confusion, and infinite numbers of People to be seen ...'[14]

Yet notwithstanding the splendour of Agra and the scale of the building operations which he had undertaken there, Shah Jahan resolved to found a new capital city at Delhi; he was partly influenced perhaps by the fact that the summer heat of Agra can be particularly trying. The location of this seventh city of Delhi, Shahjahanabad or Old Delhi (cf. map page 12), as it is now universally called, was just north of Kotla Firuz Shah and included within its limits part of the area formerly belonging to Firuzabad, the fifth Delhi built by Firuz Shah Tughluq in the second half of the fourteenth century. From the ruins of Firuzabad, as well as from buildings in the neighbourhood of the Purana Qala, Shah Jahan obtained much of the material for the walls and gateways of his new city.

The principal artery of Shahjahanabad was the famous Chandni-Chowk, which extended from the open ground in front of the Red Fort due west to the Fatehpuri Masjid (constructed in 1650 by one of Shah Jahan's wives) and then along one side of the mosque to the Lahore Gate of the city. In the seventeenth century, and indeed up to the British period, Chandni-Chowk was lined with trees and in the centre was a channel of running water so that in appearance it must have closely resembled the Chahar-Bagh in Isfahan, laid out a few years earlier. The source of the water which supplied the conduit in Chandni-Chowk and also the watercourses of the Red Fort has an interesting history. In the late fourteenth century Firuz Shah Tughluq dug a canal on the west side of Delhi extending as far as Hissar which then fell into disuse after Timur's invasion and the breakdown of centralized authority during the fifteenth century. When, however, Shah Jahan decided to restore Delhi to its former importance he commissioned his Persian favourite, Ali Mardan Khan, who had experience of canal systems at Kandahar and on the Ravi near Lahore, to repair Firuz Shah Tughluq's canal and to enlarge it by bringing a new branch from Karnal to Shahjahanabad, thereby providing the city with an alternative to its existing supply of water from the Jumna. These works were later incorporated into the nineteenth-century Rohtak and Western-Jumna Canal systems.

Some way south of Chandni-Chowk Shah Jahan constructed the imposing Jami Masjid (1644–58) (cf. pls. 85, 115) which must rank only a little behind the Taj Mahal itself as one of the finest monuments erected during his reign. Built upon a lofty platform commanding a magnificent view of the surrounding city and the Red Fort to the east, the Delhi Jami Masjid is the largest congregational mosque in northern India. Its central courtyard is 325 feet square and is surrounded on three sides by cloisters and on the fourth by a decorated prayer-hall flanked by two tall minarets and supporting three cupolas similar in shape to the dome of the Taj Mahal.

70 Taj Mahal, Agra. Part of the marble screen surrounding the tombs of Shah Jahan and Mumtaz Mahal.

71 Taj Mahal, Agra. Entrance gateway.

72 Taj Mahal, Agra. Entrance gateway. Detail of the door.

73 Part of a woollen rug made during the reign of Shah Jahan (1627–57). The complete rug is 1.85 × 3.95 m. *Bequest of Benjamin Altman, 1913, Metropolitan Museum of Art, New York.*

The heart of the empire and the principal residence of every emperor from Shah Jahan to the last of the line, Bahadur Shah II, the famous Red Fort or Lal Qala was built on the north-eastern side of Shahjahanabad close to the old fort of Salimgarh and the bridge of boats across the river. In its heyday in the seventeenth century the Red Fort constituted not only the residence of the emperor and his court but also housed the central administrative machinery of the empire, a military garrison, an arsenal, the imperial treasury, factories (*karkhaneh*) for the manufacture of luxury commodities, and much else besides (cf. pls. 86, 87, 113, 116).

The harem alone, which lay in the south-eastern part of the Fort, must have covered a quite considerable area of which nothing now remains apart from one or two pavilions. While the first and foremost function of the Mughul harem was, of course, to provide maximum privacy and security for the emperor's wives and concubines, it inevitably acquired other functions inherent in such a peculiar institution. At any one time the harem contained not only the four legal wives and the reigning favourites but also aging women discarded years before as well as survivors from previous reigns, queens or concubines of the emperor's father or grandfather, widows and unmarried sisters, together with numerous cousins and distant female relatives. To these must be added the emperor's children of both sexes, acquiring at an early age jealous animosities towards half-brothers and half-sisters; a large number of female servants some of whom acted as guards and others as paid spies; and the eunuchs – for whose favours, however inadequate, women starved of sexual satisfaction by the sheer number of contestants for their master's favour hungrily competed. The basic administration of such a household (Abul Fazl mentions 5,000 women in Akbar's harem), the provision of food, dress and other necessities, the payment of carefully graded allowances, the maintenance of discipline and attendance to the constant requirements of its inhabitants must have been a very considerable undertaking about which next to nothing is known.

Apart from the harem and the pavilions reserved for the emperor's private use, much of the interior of the Red Fort was designed to provide accommodation for the conduct of public business, such as the reception of foreign ambassadors, the proclamation of war and peace and the emperor's personal administration of justice. Here too were located the establishments of the *vakil* or Chief Minister, the *vazir* or Finance Minister (sometimes known as the *diwan*) and the *mir bakhshi* or Minister of War, the three most important officials of the empire, together with a number of less important branches of the administration. The *amirs*, the military backbone of the regime, were also to be found in regular attendance at the Red Fort in their role as an imperial nobility which gave service to the emperor. The racial composition of this nobility was extremely diverse although the principal groups were clearly distinguishable: Turks and Persians whose ancestors had entered India with the Mughuls or who had been tempted to seek service at the Mughul court by the prospect of wealth and high office; Afghans, many of whom were descended from families long-established in India, who tended to regard the Mughuls as interlopers; native-born Muslims, descendants of converts or of Turkish invaders who had entered the sub-continent generations before and who had acquired Indian wives and ways; and Rajputs whose fathers or grandfathers had been drawn into the imperial orbit by Akbar's far-sighted policy of Mughul-Rajput partnership. To these were added, in the second half of the seventeenth century, Deccani Muslims and Marathas as the frontiers of the empire pressed steadily southwards.

Divided by race, religion, language and manners, the Mughul nobility consti- tuted a microcosm of the empire itself, with Hindu pitted against Muslim, Shia

74 Taj Mahal, Agra. Detail of the decoration in semi-precious stones on the marble screen surrounding the tombs of Shah Jahan and Mumtaz Mahal.

75 Carved rock crystal bowl, probably Agra work. Mid-17th century. *Victoria and Albert Museum, London*, 986-1875. (*Height* 8.2 cm. *Diameter* 12.8 cm.)

76 Jahangir's wine-cup, formerly two-handled, with an incised inscription inlaid with white cement, c. 1605–27. *Victoria and Albert Museum, London*, I.M.152-1924. (*Height* 1.8 cm.)

77 Jade drinking vessel made for Shah Jahan in the shape of a shell and with a curved handle ter- minating in the head of an ibex. 1657. *Victoria and Albert Museum, London*, I.S.12-1962. (*Height* 5.7 cm. *Length* 18.4 cm.)

78 Two-handled carved crystal bowl. 17th century. *Victoria and Albert Museum, London*, 02608 I.S. (*Height* 5.7 cm. *Width* 14.4 cm.)

79 Oval box in rock crystal, set with rubies and emeralds in gold and mounted with silver gilt. 17th century. *Victoria and Albert Museum, London*. (*Height* 8.2 cm. *Length* 12.8 cm. *Width* 10 cm.)

80 Jade wine-vessel, with enamel set in gold. 17th century. *Victoria and Albert Museum, London*, 02594 I.S. (*Height* 11.3 cm. *Width with spout* 15 cm.)

81 Rock crystal cup. 17th century. *Victoria and Albert Museum, London*. (*Height* 5.7 cm. *Length* 12.8 cm.)

82 Agra Fort. A covered passage-way leading into the Khass Mahal (the private apart- ments of the emperor).

83 Agra Fort. The Diwan-i Am or Hall of Public Audience, looking towards the Moti Masjid or Pearl Mosque.

75

76

77

78

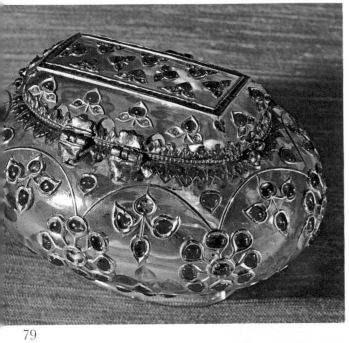

79

80

81

82
83

88

Persian against Sunni Turk, and both against Indian-born Muslims. Yet despite all this diversity there were elements in the situation which contributed to a reduction of tensions: an interest on the part of most members of the Mughul nobility in preserving a political order so beneficial to themselves (this would seem less true by the end of the century); loyalty to the Timurid dynasty which, from the seventeenth century onwards, acquired a potent charismatic influence as the fount of sovereignty and legitimate authority throughout the greater part of the subcontinent; the emergence of a genuine Mughul civilization which combined indigenous Indian with extraneous Middle Eastern and Central Asian elements and thereby helped to smooth over communal and regional antagonisms; and the Persian language which could be easily mastered (unlike Chaghatai Turkish, the language spoken *en famille* by the ruling dynasty) and which already had behind it several centuries of use in the Delhi Sultanate.

It was the genius of Akbar which transformed his followers from a loosely-knit military aristocracy into a tightly-controlled imperial bureaucracy in which, willy-nilly, anyone of consequence became a servant of the state. Thus, although the Mughul nobleman was almost always a soldier, he was frequently called upon to function as a civil administrator – in the same way as, in later times, the East India Company's military officers could be seconded to district administration or the Political service – while his rank (*mansab*) and emoluments were determined by the number of troops (between ten and ten thousand) which he was required to maintain upon a war-footing, the grading of *mansabs* in multiples of ten being taken from the military system of Chingiz Khan. The *mansabdar* sometimes received his salary in cash (the usual practice during Akbar's reign) but more often in the form of a temporary grant of an estate, district or province called a *jagir*, the size of which was determined by the rank of the *mansabdar*. The *mansabdar* collected the land revenue on his *jagir* on behalf of the government but retained a surplus to cover his expenses, to pay for the maintenance of his troops and to provide his salary. A *jagir* was rarely allowed to remain long in the hands of the same person and the assignee was often transferred to a new one after two or three years, in order to prevent the growth of local ties and loyalties which might have contributed to the emergence of hereditary interests in a particular locality.

So long as it functioned efficiently the *mansabdari* system, by reserving for the *mansabdars* as a class a dominant role in the administration, provided the empire with a comparatively stable political framework although its economic effects were ultimately to prove deleterious. For the *mansabdars* as individuals, however, it had its disadvantages. Strictly graded according to rank and subject to frequent interference from the emperor's fiscal officers in matters relating to their salaries and *jagirs*, they enjoyed their privileged status primarily as government servants and were entirely dependent upon the favour of the court for the retention of their *jagirs* or for promotion. For those who were not chieftains in their own right, like the great Rajput feudatories, the withdrawal of a *jagir* might mean ruin.

Except when absent on government business in the provinces, attendance at court was compulsory and when a *mansabdar* was transferred from one province to another he was required to present himself at the seat of government before proceeding to his new assignment; to be forbidden to appear was a mark of the emperor's extreme displeasure. Akbar, with his pronounced Persian attitude towards kingship, even demanded from his courtiers the act of prostration (*sijda*) performed at the courts of the ancient kings of Iran, a practice resented as blasphemous by the proud Afghans and the Turks from Central Asia (although Balban in the thirteenth century had also demanded it) and which Shah Jahan abolished.

84   Jami Masjid, Agra. This congregational mosque was built in 1648 for Jahan-Ara, favourite daughter of Shah Jahan.

85   Jami Masjid, Delhi.

86   Red Fort, Delhi. The Diwan-i Khass or Hall of Private Audience.

87   Red Fort, Delhi. The Lahore Gate, protected by Aurangzeb's barbican.

88   Red Fort, Delhi. The Moti Masjid, built by Aurangzeb for his private prayer, seen from the Diwan-i Khass.

89   Detail of a satin coat, embroidered with silks in chain-stitch. First half of the 17th century. *Victoria and Albert Museum, London.*

The Red Fort provided the setting for all this elaborate ceremonial, the *amirs* and those privileged to be received in audience by the emperor entering the Fort by the Lahore Gate on elephants or on horseback and then dismounting at the entrance to the Naqqar-Khana or Drum House where a military band played on days of public rejoicing and which gave access to the inner part of the palace and to the emperor's private apartments. No one was permitted to pass beyond that point except on foot and the chroniclers record with some surprise the exceptional circumstance of a reception by Aurangzeb of the exiled ruler of Kashgar, Abdullah Khan, who was carried beyond the Naqqar-Khana in a *palki* (palanquin). The Naqqar-Khana opened on to an extensive courtyard at the far end of which stood the Diwan-i Am or Hall of Public Audience where the principal *mansabdars* waited on the emperor twice daily, unless excused on grounds of urgent business or ill-health. The lesser *mansabdars* and subordinate officials stood in front of the hall according to rank and contemporary sources suggest that there were three distinct enclosures marked by red, silver and golden barriers – the latter presumably fencing off the hall itself. Every nobleman had an allotted place according to the grade of his *mansab*. To stand other than in one's proper place or to attempt to leave the durbar without permission resulted in serious punishment. On a much less formal occasion in Agra during his father's lifetime, Aurangzeb left Shah Jahan's presence without obtaining prior permission and for this offence was forbidden to approach his father for seven months. It is not difficult to imagine, therefore, the wrath which irregular behaviour among lesser folk would incur.

While the nobility stood in order of precedence inside and in front of the Diwan-i Am, the emperor was seated on a throne entered from behind the hall and raised some ten to twelve feet above the ground, thereby making attempts at assassination in open durbar virtually impossible. In front of the throne but at ground-level was placed a marble dais upon which the *vakil* sat and from this position he dealt with petitions and the public business of the day, under the emperor's direction.

Immediately behind the Diwan-i Am lay the private world of gardens and pavilions which covered all the eastern portion of the Fort and offered the imperial family that seclusion denied to them whenever they left its walls amid a vast entourage of servants and retainers. Only the most privileged *amirs*, ambassadors, foreign princelings and the favourites of the imperial family were permitted here, where the emperor received his grandees in the exquisite Diwan-i Khass or Hall of Private Audience (cf. pls. 86, 124) in which stood the *takht-i tavus*, the celebrated jewel-encrusted Peacock Throne.

The daily reception in the Diwan-i Am must have been a very splendid affair but the splendour was immeasurably enhanced on those days marked out by the court for special rejoicing: the anniversary of the emperor's birthday and accession to the throne, the *Nuruz* (the Persian New Year celebrations introduced by Akbar and subsequently abolished by Aurangzeb), the birth of an imperial prince or princess, the recovery of the emperor from an illness or the announcement of a great victory. Such occasions were used for rewarding those officials who had served the emperor with conspicuous loyalty and for showing marks of favour to those with whom he was especially pleased. Rewards might take the form of money, jewelry, weapons, horses or elephants but the commonest present was a *khilat* (a robe of honour) which at this period was often embroidered with gold thread and precious stones. The granting of standards and honorific titles was another way of rewarding faithful service, the titles consisting of sonorous phrases such as *Khan-i Khanan* ('Khan of Khans'), *Khan-i Jahan* ('Khan of the World') or *Nizam ul-Mulk* ('Regulator of the State'). Perhaps the most sought-after favour was

Fig. 14 Jade cup of greenish-white jade made for Timur's grandson, Ulugh Beg, ruler of Samarqand (1409–46), and subsequently the property of Jahangir and Shah Jahan whose names and titles are inscribed upon it. *Calouste Gulbenkian Foundation, Oeiras.*

90 Musamman Burj, Agra Fort, looking towards the Taj Mahal.

91 Musamman Burj, Agra Fort. It was from this structure that the women of the imperial harem watched elephant-fights and other entertainments and it was here that the emperor made his daily ceremonial appearance, known as *darshan*, before his subjects.

the almost royal right of beating kettle-drums and even when this rare privilege was granted it was never allowed to be exercised within a certain radius of the emperor's presence. Early in the eighteenth century a rebellious nobleman indicated that he had thrown off his allegiance simply by beating kettle-drums as he entered Delhi while, towards the close of the previous century, Aurangzeb repeatedly reprimanded his eldest son, then governor of Kabul and later to become the Emperor Bahadur Shah I, for appropriating to himself the prerogatives of royalty while his father was still alive. Aurangzeb complained that, in addition to beating kettle-drums, his son was reported to have sat in the durbar on a carpet raised above the surrounding carpets on which the members of his entourage and his senior advisers were seated, to have erected a screen in the congregational mosque in Kabul so that he could perform his daily prayers unobserved, and to have staged elephant-fights. A favourite spectacle at the Mughul court, elephant-fights were the prerogative of the emperor alone and the chroniclers frequently quote cases of recalcitrant *amirs* and rebellious sons staging these contests as proof of their evil intentions.

During the seventeenth century, however, only a small minority among the *mansabdars* of the empire seriously contemplated the overthrow of the established order. For most of those who stood daily before the Diwan-i Am the gift of a *khilat* or a small sum of money was a sufficient proof of favour to enhance their prestige among their fellows and support their credit with the Delhi bankers upon whose credulity much of their finery not infrequently depended. The Mughul nobleman did not normally possess hereditary estates as a source of income or as a sanctuary to which he could retire when his extravagance caught up with him and his *jagir* could be removed at a moment's notice – and often was. Moreover, as the century advanced his economic position steadily deteriorated as he was now compelled to expend a considerable part of his income on gifts to the emperor, a degrading practice forced upon Shah Jahan and Aurangzeb by the cost of their campaigns in the Deccan and which had the effect of making all but the greatest nobles even more dependent upon the favour of the court.

There were always, however, refractory exceptions and even during the period between 1556 and 1712, when the empire was generally in the hands of able and active rulers, the Mughul nobility required tactful as well as firm handling in the atmosphere of perpetual intrigue surrounding the imperial family and the absence of a clear-cut law of succession to the throne. Much of the potential danger could be neutralized by the regular transfer of offices and *jagirs* and by playing off mutually antagonistic factions against each other but unpredictable outbreaks of violence still occurred which sometimes demanded very considerable efforts to suppress. The inherent turbulence of the ruling class, coupled with the ambitions of younger sons and brothers of the emperor, therefore necessitated the establishment of an elaborate system of espionage which included the stationing, in all the principal towns, of news-writers who acted as the emperor's eyes and ears. Aurangzeb, pathologically suspicious of members of his own family, extended the system by paying women in his sons' harems to report their every word.

During a reign of thirty years Shah Jahan was confronted by little overt hostility from his *mansabdars*, notwithstanding his extravagance, his loss of prestige following the disastrous expeditions to Balkh and Kandahar, and his growing tendency to idle away his time in Delhi or Agra, delegating excessive authority in the provinces to his sons and to the most trusted of his *amirs*. To the Europeans who visited Agra or Delhi during his reign, his court represented the acme of oriental splendour, wealth and unfettered absolutism. Few who had seen the

92 Khass Mahal, Agra Fort. The Khass Mahal contained the private apartments of the emperor. The garden in front, known as the Anguri-Bagh, was surrounded on the remaining three sides by accommodation reserved for members of the emperor's harem.

93 Musamman Burj, Agra Fort. Marble screening.

94 Part of a ceremonial girdle (*patka*) of painted cotton, formerly in the possession of the Nizams of Hyderabad. Late 17th or early 18th century. The complete girdle is 5.2 × 0.61 m. *Victoria and Albert Museum, London.*

emperor at the height of his power, seated in the Diwan-i Am before his assembled grandees, could have predicted that his last days would be so utterly tragic.

From an early age Shah Jahan's four sons, Dara Shukoh, Shah Shuja, Aurangzeb, and Murad Bakhsh (cf. pl. 62) had grown up in an atmosphere of bitter rivalry, despite the fact that all were children of the same mother, Mumtaz Mahal. In 1657 Shah Jahan was taken seriously ill and the expectation of his early death provoked all four into making a desperate bid for the throne. Only two candidates, however, stood much chance of success: Dara Shukoh (cf. pl. 63), already forty-two, and Aurangzeb (cf. fig. 16, page 121), who was thirty-nine. Dara Shukoh, his father's favourite and heir, was a man of broad intellectual interests, a Sufi and an eclectic in religion who had translated the Upanishads into Persian. With these accomplishments, however, went an arrogant manner and a high-handedness which provoked resentment among those whose support he most needed. Also well-educated but conspicuously lacking any intellectual curiosity for subjects beyond the traditional spectrum of Islamic studies, Aurangzeb combined strict religious orthodoxy with an acute sense of political realism and a fierce appetite for power. Personally less attractive than Dara Shukoh, he was his superior in both military talent and administrative ability.

In the conflict which raged amongst the brothers between 1657 and 1659 Aurangzeb easily out-classed the rest. In due course Dara Shukoh was captured, paraded through the streets of Delhi under humiliating circumstances and then executed (he is buried in Humayun's tomb). Shah Shuja, a fugitive in Arakan, was murdered by pirates. Murad Bakhsh, induced to surrender by assurances that he would come to no harm, was first imprisoned in Salimgarh beside the Red Fort and then in Gwalior where he was murdered, together with Dara Shukoh's son, Sulaiman Shukoh. As early as the summer of 1658 Aurangzeb held a coronation durbar in the Shalimar-Bagh outside Delhi on the Karnal road, probably in order to strengthen the morale of his supporters, but it was not until the summer of 1659 that a second and more splendid ceremony was performed in the Red Fort at which the new emperor assumed the title of Alamgir – 'World-Conqueror'.

But Shah Jahan was still alive. Grown helpless with old age, poor health and the onset of senility, he was no more than a spectator at the savage contest between his sons and the emergence of Aurangzeb, never a favourite child, as undisputed victor led to his own imprisonment in the Agra Fort where he survived for seven more years until 1666, tended by his eldest daughter, Jahan-Ara. On his death-bed he is said to have kept his eyes fixed on the Taj Mahal, clearly visible from the apartments to which he was confined, and there he was subsequently buried beside his long-dead queen.

Thus ended in a grim twilight the reign which saw the Mughul Empire attain, at least superficially, unsurpassed splendour and opulence. Indeed it was the glittering facade of Shah Jahan's court which seemed to confirm the reports of India's inexhaustible riches for the European traders and adventurers who were soon to make themselves felt on the fringes of the empire. Less than a century separates the death of Shah Jahan from Plassey, Buxar, and the grant of the *diwani* of Bengal, Bihar and Orissa to the East India Company.

Fig. 15 Portrait of a Mughul lady inscribed with the name of Gul Safa, a concubine of Dara Shukoh. Painting by Rai Anup Chattar, c. 1640–50. *Johnson 13. 9, India Office Library, London.*

Aurangzeb and the Decline of Imperial Delhi

1657–1761

Fig. 16   Engraving of Aurangzeb
by de l'Armessin, 1680. *Cabinet des
Estampes OD. 51. fo. 8a,
Bibliothèque Nationale, Paris.*

Of all the able men who have sat upon the throne of Delhi no name evokes an image of such sombre grandeur as does that of Aurangzeb whose long reign, beginning with his second coronation in 1659 and ending with his death in 1707, stretches across almost half a century of Indian history.

In his early years he had craved for power as some men crave for wine or women, although as a young man he had not been altogether without more attractive failings. There is, for example, the well-attested story of his infatuation with a concubine of his maternal aunt's husband, the beautiful Zainabadi, from the suburb of Zainabad across the Tapti from Burhanpur where he first set eyes upon her in his aunt's garden. Although accounts of the scandal differ, one source relates how Aurangzeb exchanged her for a concubine from his own harem and thereafter was so enamoured with her that he even agreed to drink wine at her insistence and was on the point of putting the forbidden cup to his lips when Zainabadi, whose good sense obviously exceeded her vanity, snatched it away. The Venetian adventurer, Manucci, gives a spiteful version of this incident which may nonetheless contain a germ of truth:

'Aurangzeb grew very fond of one of the dancing-women in his harem, and through the great love he bore to her he neglected for some time his prayers and his austerities, filling up his days with music and dances; and going even farther, he enlivened himself with wine, which he drank at the instance of the said dancing-girl. The dancer died, and Aurangzeb made a vow never to drink wine again nor to listen to music. In after-days he was accustomed to say that God had been very gracious to him by putting an end to that dancing-girl's life, by reason of whom he had committed so many iniquities, and had run the risk of never reigning through being occupied in vicious practices.' [15]

Aurangzeb's treatment of his brothers has attracted almost universal condemnation but there can be little doubt that, even if ambition and superior ability had not prompted him to make a bid for the throne, he would have been compelled to act as he did if he were not to suffer the very same fate which he meted out to them. In Mughul dynastic disputes it was a case of kill or be killed, but his harsh treatment of his father is harder to justify. The fact that Shah Jahan survived as a prisoner until 1666 compelled Aurangzeb, during those first seven years of the reign, to purchase the loyalty of his father's *amirs* by undertaking aggressive frontier campaigns which would provide plunder, *jagirs* and honours for any who might be inclined to doubt that in energy and will-power the new emperor far out-stripped his predecessor. The results of this policy, however, proved far from gratifying. The campaigns went badly, the Jats rebelled, the north-west frontier broke into revolt, the Maratha problem remained as intractable as ever; all this notwithstanding the fact that the emperor himself was a seasoned administrator and military commander who could call upon the assistance of such able advisers as his uncle, Shayista Khan, the brother of Mumtaz Mahal, and Mir Jumla, the wily Isfahani diamond-merchant who had betrayed the Qutb-Shah of Golconda to enter the Mughul service. During this period Aurangzeb was still very far from being the religious recluse which he was later to become. In Delhi he maintained his court very much as his father and grandfather had done; like them he celebrated the Persian *Nuruz* and was publicly weighed against gold coins or precious stones, and at the instance of his favourite sister, Roshan-Ara, travelled up to Kashmir with an enormous entourage at the onset of the hot weather. At first, too, he employed the Rajput chieftains side by side with Muslims in some of the highest offices of state, in exactly the same way as his predecessors had done.

A change of direction became apparent, however, after Shah Jahan's death in 1666 removed the danger of an attempted restoration of his father to the throne and thereafter Aurangzeb struck out along new paths, his aim being to destroy the traditional non-communal foundations of the Mughul Empire and to restore the orthodox Muslim character of what had always been, in theory at least, an orthodox Muslim State. In pursuing these objectives Aurangzeb was responding, perhaps unconsciously, to a powerful impulse felt by a number of far-seeing leaders of the Muslim community who were perturbed by the implications of Akbar's heterodox approach to the problems of imperial government in a plural society such as that of Mughul India. Since the first decades of the seventeenth century a reaction had been gaining ground among orthodox believers against what seemed to them to be the gradual submersion of Indian Islam in a morass of doctrinal latitudinarianism and in the ever-encroaching miasma of Hindu influences. The emperor's attitude, however, was to prove fatal for the future of the empire since it led to the total alienation of the Rajput element in the imperial service because of his policy of discrimination which reached its climax in 1679 with the reimposition of the hated *jizya*, the poll-tax on non-Muslims abolished by Akbar. This alienation of the Rajputs brought about a profound change in the character of the Mughul Empire, a change reflected in the growing rigidity of the emperor's already severely orthodox approach to the problems of imperial government. His determination to complete the annexation of the independent Sultanates in the south, begun years before when he had been his father's viceroy in the Deccan, proved too formidable a task even for his iron will-power and immense resources. It was this futile exercise in aggression which finally led him to quit Delhi, much to the disgust of the court, for a wandering life in the camps and garrison-towns beyond the Narbada. He never again returned to the north, dying in Ahmadnagar in 1707.

Under Aurangzeb the Mughul Empire reached its greatest extent, yet the emperor's puritanical outlook and his costly wars meant that the generous encouragement given by his predecessors to the arts and learning was almost completely withdrawn. By temperament an ascetic who avoided all forms of luxury and ostentation and even refused to wear silk against his body, Aurangzeb regarded both music and the representational arts as sinful, while his taste in literature was restricted to works of theology and poetry of a devotional or didactic character. He had none of his father's passion for architecture and in Delhi itself only a very few buildings are associated with his name, for instance the two massive barbicans protecting the gateways of the Red Fort (cf. pl. 87) and the exquisite Moti Masjid (cf. pl. 88) inside the palace, built to provide the emperor with a place for private prayer. Associated with female members of the imperial family is the elegant Zinat al-Masjid in Daryaganj, built by Aurangzeb's second daughter, Zinat al-Nisa, and not completed until the following reign, as well as the delicate brick and plaster mausoleum of his sister, Roshan-Ara, in the Roshan-Ara-Bagh in Sabzimandi.

95 Miniature: A turkey cock. Painting by Mansur, 1612. *Victoria and Albert Museum, London*, I.M. 135-1921. (23.5 × 16.3 cm.)

96 Miniature: Aurangzeb as an old man performing his *namaz*, the Muslim act of prayer. Late 17th century. *Property of the author* (25 × 16 cm.)

97 Miniature: The lovers' bed. From a manuscript of the *Svadhinapathika Nayika*. Second half of the 17th century. *British Museum, London*. (20 × 26.5 cm.)

98 Miniature: Farrukhsiyar (1713-9). c. 1750-60. *Victoria and Albert Museum, London*, I.M.102-1922. (44.2 × 28.8 cm.)

99 Miniature: Bahadur Shah II (1837-58) with attendants. First half of the 19th century. *Property of Dr Percival Spear.* (22 × 31.5 cm.)

100 A jade hookah-bowl, with precious stones set in gold. 18th century but partly reset at a later date. *Victoria and Albert Museum, London*, 02593 I.S. (*Height* 19 cm. *Diameter* 17.7 cm.)

101 Jade bowl, with precious stones set in gold. 18th century. *Victoria and Albert Museum, London*, 02564 I.S. (*Height* 6.9 cm. *Width* 16.9 cm.)

102 Translucent white jade cup with silver fittings. *Victoria and Albert Museum, London*, 903-1873. (*Height* 7.5 cm. *Width with handle* 16.3 cm.)

دربار بهادرشاه پادشاه

100

101

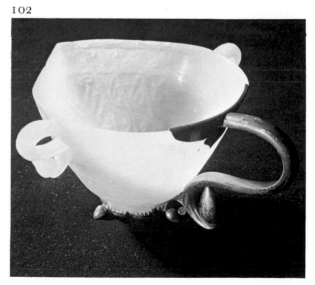

102

103

104 105

106

107

108

109

110

111

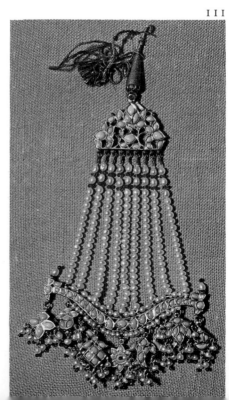

Roshan-Ara died in 1671 but she had laid out the garden years before at the time when her father was completing his new capital of Shahjahanabad. It is a matter of the greatest regret that her tomb-chamber and the once-lovely garden surrounding it should have been for so long neglected that they are now in an advanced state of decay.

Yet despite Aurangzeb's personal hostility to the arts and his removal of the seat of government to the south, Delhi remained the foremost city of the empire. Many of the Mughul grandees (now far more Indianized than their grandfathers and great-grandfathers who had served Akbar or Jahangir) were detained for long periods in the Deccan by the side of their master but they continued to maintain their residences in the city where their families and households employed the services of the best artists, craftsmen and entertainers which money could buy. Early in his reign the emperor had appointed *muhtasibs* (censors of morals) to enforce traditional Islamic standards of public behaviour, but all to no effect. The musicians and singers, dancers and courtesans of late seventeenth-century Delhi still had few equals and those who frequented their company cared little for the injunctions of their distant sovereign, a frail figure (cf. pl. 96), often bent in prayer, earning his daily bread by making copies of the Quran, and examining every detail of an administrative machine grown increasingly cumbrous with the passing years. While Aurangzeb wrestled with the problem of the ubiquitous Marathas and the intransigent politics of the south, life in Delhi continued in much the same way as it had always done and it is unlikely that when the news of the old man's death reached the city there was much display of grief – or much surprise when it became known that his sons were already locked in a life-and-death struggle to decide who should succeed him.

The victor, Bahadur Shah, was already elderly. A tried soldier, an able, moderate man, he had lived most of his life overshadowed by his awe-inspiring father and as governor of Kabul had, on more than one occasion, revealed his impatience at being so long deprived of real authority. Had he come to the throne younger or had he lived longer it is probable that he would have left a more positive mark upon the history of the period than his brief reign between 1707 and 1712 permitted. To the inhabitants of Delhi he was almost a total stranger; it is unlikely that he ever resided within the Red Fort during his five years as emperor and it was said of him that he had spent so much of his life under canvas that he hated sleeping in an enclosed room.

During the reigns of Aurangzeb and Bahadur Shah the capital of the empire had been neglected by its masters but under Bahadur Shah's feeble successors Delhi once again became an active political centre such as it had hardly been since Shah Jahan had been overthrown amid the rivalries of his sons. Paradoxically, it was the weakness of the Mughul rulers of the early eighteenth century, the disintegration of the imperial administration and the emergence of new forces within the empire (Jats, Sikhs and Marathas) which gave Delhi its renewed importance as the place where emperors could be made and unmade, titles and honours granted, provinces allotted or transferred. With the death of Bahadur Shah the court nobility emerged as the principal usurpers of imperial authority and the history of the next decade was decided by the ambitions of such powerful figures as Zulfiqar Khan Bahadur, the leader of the Persian and Shia faction at court, and his Sunni rival, Asaf Jah, whose family originated in Bukhara and who was later, as the first Nizam, to found the independent Asaf Jahi dynasty in Hyderabad. Another influential group was headed by a Muslim family long established in India, the Sayyids of Barha in Uttar Pradesh who claimed the right to command the vanguard of the imperial

103 Jade box, with precious stones set in gold. 18th century. *Victoria and Albert Museum, London,* 02539 I.S. (*Height* 2.5 cm. *Width* 17.5 cm.)

104 Gold necklace set with jargoons, emeralds and pearls, and enamelled. 18th century. *Victoria and Albert Museum, London,* 03202 I.S. (*Height* 19 cm. *Width* 17.7 cm.)

105 Sword-handle in the form of a horse's head; mottled jade inlaid with gold and set with precious stones. 18th century. *Victoria and Albert Museum, London,* I.S. 100-1955. (*Height* 13.2 cm. *Width* 7.5 cm.)

106 Gold armlet, enamelled and set with plate diamonds. 18th century. *Victoria and Albert Museum, London,* 03148 I.S. (*Length* 10 cm. *Width* 3.6 cm.)

107 Spinel ruby pendant, uncut, polished and drilled, and engraved with the names of Akbar, Jahangir, Shah Jahan and Aurangzeb. *Victoria and Albert Museum, London,* I.M. 243-1922. (133 carats. *Length* 3 cm.)

108 Gold bracelet, enamelled and set with jargoons. 18th century. *Victoria and Albert Museum, London,* 03311 I.S. (*Diameter* 7.5 cm.)

109 Tooled and enamelled gold thumb ring, set with rubies and emeralds. Early 18th century. Lucknow. *Victoria and Albert Museum, London,* I.M.707-1920. (*Length* 3.2 cm. *Width* 2.9 cm.)

110 Jade pendant of a necklace, set with rubies and emeralds in gold. 18th century. *Victoria and Albert Museum, London,* 02535 I.S. (*Height* 7.5 cm. *Width* 5 cm.)

111 Gold head-ornament, enamelled and set with turquoises and pearls. 18th century. *Victoria and Albert Museum, London,* 03181 I.S. (*Height* 15 cm. *Width* 10 cm.)

army and against whom, famed for their courage and their recklessness, Aurangzeb had long before warned his successors. In 1712 the family was headed by two brothers, Husayn Ali, deputy-governor of Patna, and Abdullah, governor of Allahabad.

At the bidding of these factions the four sons of Bahadur Shah, mere puppets, were compelled to take the stage and while three soon perished in the subsequent upheaval the fourth, Jahandar Shah, was raised to the throne by Zulfiqar Khan and for a few months filled the Red Fort with tumblers and dancing-girls, while all authority was concentrated in the hands of Zulfiqar Khan, now appointed *vazir*, and his father who was already *vakil-i mutlaq*. The successful ascendancy of one faction merely whetted the appetite of its rivals and in 1713 the Sayyid brothers carried out a swift *coup d'état* in which Jahandar Shah was replaced by Farrukhsiyar (cf. pl. 98), a grandson of Bahadur Shah. Jahandar Shah himself was murdered in the Naqqar-Khana of the Red Fort and his body buried in Humayun's tomb, now become a cemetery for Mughul failures, while Zulfiqar Khan was disgraced and executed at the insistence of the new emperor although perhaps against the wishes of the Sayyid brothers. Inept, cruel and vicious, Farrukhsiyar had been singled out above the other members of his family because the Sayyid brothers believed that they could bridle him easily. Here they miscalculated, however, and between 1713 and 1719 Delhi was distracted by the squabbles of the king-makers and their protégé until the former, despairing of ever effectively controlling the wayward emperor, blinded and then murdered him in the very building where his predecessor had met his end.

Despite his worthlessness, Farrukhsiyar with his dissolute, pleasure-loving ways, apparently aroused feelings of affection among the people of Delhi, and especially among the lower classes. Aurangzeb and Bahadur Shah had cared nothing for the city, but under Farrukhsiyar it became once more the home of a gay, extravagant court where patronage and employment were dispensed by an improvident emperor oblivious of all restraint. It is significant that the removal of Farrukhsiyar's body to Humayun's tomb touched off a riot in which the Sayyid brothers were reviled by the city mob for their treachery to their master.

For a few months longer, however, the king-makers maintained their position by raising two more grandsons of Bahadur Shah to the throne, but they overplayed their hand when they replaced these by a third, Muhammad Shah (1720–48) (cf. pl. 118). Without possessing any obvious talent as a ruler, Muhammad Shah's greatest asset was his capacity for survival. Intelligent, shrewd and deceitful, twenty-eight years of accumulated experience on the throne of Delhi were to give him a sharp insight into the motives of those around him, thereby helping to counter-balance the defects of an essentially negative personality. Only eighteen at his accession, he was quick to appreciate that seven years of unrestrained power had made the Sayyid brothers objects of bitter hatred and jealousy, and he therefore plunged into the congenial task of overthrowing his former patrons with the help of the Nizam, Asaf Jah, whose preoccupation with affairs in the Deccan made it unlikely that he would interfere for very long in the politics of the north. In this way Muhammad Shah rid himself of the Sayyid brothers in the first months of the reign and thereafter ruled for more than a quarter of a century without either taking any great interest in or making any positive impact upon those great events outside the immediate vicinity of Delhi which were to decide the shape of Indian history for the next half century and even longer.

Pleasure-loving and genial, a handsome man who ruled graciously over a court of poets and prostitutes, Muhammad Shah lived a life in the Red Fort outwardly

Fig. 17 Islam Khan Rumi, *subahdar* of Malwa. An example of a prominent refugee from outside India rising high in the Mughul service, Islam Khan had formerly been governor of Basra on behalf of the Ottoman Sultan but had quarrelled with his master and fled to India. He was killed in 1676 accompanying the future Emperor Bahadur Shah against Bijapur. Painting by Rai Chitarman c. 1750–60. *Johnson 1.11, India Office Library, London.*

112 The interior of Agra Fort, looking towards the Moti Masjid.

113 Red Fort, Delhi. The Hayat-Bakhsh-Bagh, a favourite garden of the later Mughul emperors in the north-eastern part of the fort.

114 Red Fort, Delhi. Detail of a marble screen in the Khass Mahal.

115 Jami Masjid, Delhi.

116 Red Fort, Delhi. A pavilion in the Hayat-Bakhsh-Bagh. On festive occasions lamps were placed in the small niches (*bottom right*) behind a cascade of running water.

little different from that of his ancestors. The splendour of the daily routine remained unchanged; there were the same formal appearances in the Diwan-i Am, the same crowded festivities, the traditional ceremonial and the old extravagance. To a generation of courtiers who passed their days in kite-flying, quail-fighting and suchlike amusements the austerities of Aurangzeb's reign must have seemed very remote. Yet the frivolity was not without its compensations. There was, admittedly, no money for building, but painters were in demand again and so were poets, whether in Persian or in Urdu, the latter language now for the first time becoming fashionable for poetry. To the greatest Urdu writer of the age were attributed the lines:

'Vali's heart has been captured by Delhi,
Let someone go and tell Muhammad Shah of it.'[16]

The silver twilight of Mughul civilization had begun and, even if power and pomp were rapidly disappearing, Delhi remained the sanctuary of an urbane, sophisticated court which still had taste, even if it lacked talent. During the two preceding centuries the city had witnessed an interchange of ideas and customs which, under Mughul rule, had taken place in camp and durbar, in library, bazaar and bordello. In Muhammad Shah's Delhi the separate strands came together, Persian court culture in its Islamic framework blending with the ancient traditions of India. No doubt those who had grown grey in the service of Aurangzeb – men such as Asaf Jah – deplored the hybrid, cosmopolitan spirit of the age but when Muhammad Shah (and Farrukhsiyar before him) attended the Holi festival of his Hindu subjects, it must have seemed as if this great-grandson of a great-grandson of Akbar was fulfilling, albeit somewhat superficially, the dream of Hindu-Muslim *rapprochement* expressed a century and a half before in the stones of Fatehpur Sikri.

The age of Muhammad Shah has a truly *fin de siècle* quality about it, although it is unlikely that during the early years of the reign a citizen of Delhi could have imagined how rapidly the end of the empire was approaching. Despite the savage rivalries of the nobility, which had scarred the turbulent second decade of the eighteenth century, life in Delhi must have continued much as it had always been since the first coming of the Mughuls and the city was very far from being the picturesque ruin it would be a hundred years later. The new centres of political and commercial power now fast rising into prominence – Murshidabad in Bengal, Poona, Hyderabad, Fyzabad and Lucknow in Oudh – offered no real competition and Delhi was still the finest place to seek one's fortune, whether as a *condottiere*, a courtesan or a poet. It was of this period that Mir wrote:

'The streets of Delhi are not mere streets, they are like the album of a painter;
Every figure I saw there was a model of perfection.'[17]

The end of this idyll was sudden and unforeseen. While Muhammad Shah was gaily wasting his years on the throne to which the Sayyids of Barha had raised him storm clouds were rising in the west. The Safavid dynasty of Iran – sometimes the ally, sometimes the rival and always the *arbiter elegantiarum* of the Mughul court – had been swept away by the Ghilzai Afghans who, between 1720 and 1730, sacked Isfahan and turned much of the country into a shambles. They were finally expelled by Nadir Shah (cf. pl. 119), one of Iran's greatest soldiers, who from 1730 until his death in 1747 pursued a career of almost ceaseless aggression against his neighbours. In January 1739 news reached Delhi that he was invading India, that first Peshawar and then Lahore had been occupied and that the governor of the

Fig. 18   Silver rupee of Nadir Shah, minted at Shajahanabad, A.H. 1152 (A.D. 1739–40). *British Museum, London. (Actual size)*

117   Red Fort, Delhi. Part of the Hayat-Bakhsh-Bagh, looking towards the Hira-Mahal, a small pavilion built by Bahadur Shah II.

118   Miniature: Muhammad Shah (1720–48) on horseback. First half of the 18th century. *British Museum, London.* (38 × 26 cm.)

119   The Persian conqueror, Nadir Shah (1736–47). Painting by an unknown artist. Middle of the 18th century. *Victoria and Albert Museum, London*, I.M.20-1919. (1.65 × 1.04 m.)

120   Miniature: Akbar Shah II (1806–37) holding a durbar in the Diwan-i Khass of the Red Fort. On the left is Sir David Ochterlony, the Company's Resident at the Mughul court, c. 1820. *India Office Library, London.* (48 × 40.5 cm.)

Panjab had given battle and had been utterly defeated. This was not an emergency for which Muhammad Shah had been prepared, either by temperament or training, but, nevertheless, he marched out of Delhi with a force of 300,000 men, 2,000 elephants and a large quantity of guns and advanced as far as Karnal in the path of the invader. Here a fortified camp was constructed and filled with the enormous quantities of gear and the horde of camp-followers which were so often the ruin of Mughul armies in the eighteenth century; and here, supported by the Nizam and his implacable enemy, Saadat Khan Burhan al-Mulk, *subahdar* of Oudh, the emperor awaited the invader. Despite a numerical superiority in men and guns, the Mughul forces were easily out-manoeuvred and out-fought by the Persians, and Muhammad Shah was forced to sue for peace. Not since Humayun had been a suppliant at the Persian court nearly two centuries before had the Mughuls experienced so complete a humiliation as when Nadir Shah, riding from his camp in the Shalimar-Bagh, entered Delhi as a conqueror and was received in the Red Fort by the emperor who proffered him jewels and treasure. That night Nadir Shah occupied the apartments built by Shah Jahan close to the Diwan-i Khass, while Muhammad Shah slept in the comparatively modest Asad-Burj on the south-west corner of the walls and the next day the Persian celebrated the *Nuruz* (which that year coincided with the *Id-i Gorban*, the Muslim 'Day of Sacrifice') in the palace of the Mughuls, the *khutba* being read in his name throughout the city.

At first the occupying army maintained some semblance of discipline but it was not long before a serious brawl occurred between the Persians and the inhabitants of the city in which an attempt was made on Nadir Shah's life. Perhaps glad of an excuse to bring to an end the uneasy truce, he immediately ordered a retaliatory massacre which he watched from the roof of the golden-domed Sunahri Masjid in Chandni-Chowk, built in 1721 by Roshan al-Dowleh, an immensely wealthy and notoriously corrupt *amir* who had played a leading part in the political in-fighting of Farrukhsiyar's and the early years of Muhammad Shah's reigns.

The loss of life and property on this occasion most probably exceeded that of Timur's sack of 1398 so that within living memory the term *nadirshahi* has been used in Delhi as synonymous with a disaster of the greatest magnitude. Beginning early in the morning and lasting until sunset, a whole day was devoted to murder, rape, plunder and arson. Then followed the sealing of the granaries while the surrounding villages were systematically looted of their grain and the principal citizens were tortured to reveal the hiding-places of their wealth, an operation which produced three crores of, or thirty-million, rupees. For eight weeks the city suffered indescribable misery and many who survived the fury of Nadir Shah's soldiers died of disease or starvation. The booty included the treasures accumulated by the Mughuls since Babur's defeat of Sultan Ibrahim, the Peacock Throne itself, priceless stones such as the *Koh-i Nur* and the *Darya-ye Nur*, jewelry, *objets d'art*, fine arms and accoutrements, books and manuscripts and immense sums in cash, while the stables were emptied of their elephants, horses and camels. Finally the hapless emperor was forced to cede to his conqueror Sind, Kabul and the districts west of the Indus. Nadir Shah then withdrew, taking with him all that remained of the tangible glory of the Mughuls.

Muhammad Shah had nine more years to reign, playing his role against the back-cloth of a looted palace and a ravished city. The inhabitants of Delhi, and especially the commercial classes, had suffered appallingly in the holocaust and while they struggled to return to their old way of life parts of Delhi must have remained almost uninhabited for a decade or more. Was it, one wonders, in this

121 The governor of the Red Fort and his entourage approaching the eastern entrance of the Jami Masjid, Delhi, during the reign of Shah Alam. Drawn and engraved by Thomas Daniell, 1795. *British Museum, London.*

122 The western gateway of the Purana Qala, Delhi, built by Sher Shah Sur, c. 1540–5. Drawn and engraved by Thomas Daniell, 1796. *British Museum, London.*

123 The tomb of Humayun, Delhi, c. 1820. By an unknown Delhi artist. *India Office Library, London,* ADD.OR.1808. (53 × 71 cm.)

124 Red Fort, Delhi. The Diwan-i Khass shortly after the Mutiny. From the journal of Lt George Welby Eaton, c. 1858. *India Office Library, London,* MSS.EUR.D 512/1 fo. 40. (7.5 × 12 cm.)

121

122

125
126

127

128

grim period that Muhammad Shah laid out beside the Jumna just north of the Old City the beautiful garden known as the Qudsiya-Bagh (cf. pl. 125) in honour of Nawab Qudsiya Begum, a celebrated dancing-girl who became his mistress and later the mother of his successor, Ahmad Shah? The Qudsiya-Bagh was to remain a favourite retreat of the Mughuls for as long as the dynasty lasted.

Nadir Shah's sack of Delhi marked the real end of the Mughul Empire, although the dynasty itself, bereft of military resources and possessing pitifully slight political influence, survived for a further hundred and twenty years as a venerated anachronism. Throughout the two decades which span the middle years of the century the fate of India was being decided far away from Delhi: by the Marathas, who ever since the time of Baji Rao the Great Peshwa (1720–40), had been expanding steadily northwards at the expense of the old Mughul *subahs* of Central India; by the Muslim rulers of Oudh and Hyderabad; and by an unpredictable *deus ex machina* in the person of Ahmad Shah Durrani, a former protégé of Nadir Shah. An Afghan chieftain, he had carved out for himself an extensive kingdom comprising present-day Afghanistan, much of eastern Iran, Sind, Kashmir and the Panjab, and was thus in a position to intervene decisively in the affairs of northern India. In 1757 he delivered Delhi over to all the horrors of a sack only a little less destructive than that commanded by Nadir Shah, while in 1761 he achieved the greatest triumph of his career when he crushed the forces of the Maratha confederacy at the third battle of Panipat.

The threat of Maratha raids or sudden incursions by Afghan armies from beyond the Indus were, however, no more than brief passing events in the story of eighteenth-century Delhi. The main preoccupation at the Mughul court continued to be survival in times of change and upheaval. A protector close at hand had become imperative but Ahmad Shah Durrani, preoccupied with his far-flung possessions and unreliable at the best of times, was far from suitable in a role which fell more naturally to the Nawab-Vazirs of Oudh. Persians from Khurasan, this talented dynasty provided a rallying point for Shiism in the sub-continent as well as a refuge for scholars and men of letters, so that their capital, Lucknow (which finally superseded Fyzabad in 1775), eventually replaced Delhi as the home of the most polished Urdu. The founder of the line, Saadat Khan Burhan al-Mulk, had been appointed *subahdar* of Oudh by Muhammad Shah as early as 1724 and had thereafter ruled the province as a virtually independent sovereign. He had fought and negotiated with Nadir Shah at Karnal and had committed suicide shortly afterwards. He had been succeeded as *subahdar* by his nephew, Safdar Jang, a man of even greater vigour and ability who, following the death of Muhammad Shah in 1748, had been appointed *vazir* by the new emperor, Ahmad Shah (1748–54). Utterly undistinguished as a ruler, Ahmad Shah contributed nothing either good or bad to the history of his age and it was left to Safdar Jang to try to chart a safe course for the empire in those grim times when it seemed probable that the Marathas or the Afghans would sweep away the dying Mughul *raj*.

Had Safdar Jang been free to govern as he wished in the name of the emperor the story of Delhi in this period might have been very different but it was his misfortune (and even more his master's) that he encountered a rival as able as himself in Ghazi al-Din Imad al-Mulk, a grandson of Asaf Jah whose restless ambition soon found Delhi preferable to Hyderabad as a centre in which to satisfy his thirst for power. Intellectually precocious and with pretensions to scholarship, Ghazi al-Din combined a fertile, ingenious mind with a degree of savagery rare even in that age. When Safdar Jang died in 1754 Ghazi al-Din promptly seized the Emperor Ahmad Shah, blinded him and then deposed him, putting in his place an

Fig. 19 Lady holding a rose. Painting from the third quarter of the 18th century. *Johnson 13.5, India Office Library, London.*

125 Qudsiya-Bagh, Delhi, c. 1820. By an unknown artist. *India Office Library, London,* ADD.OR. 553. (26 × 36 cm.)

126 An East India Company official leaving his house, c. 1832. *India Office Library, London.* (28 × 43 cm.)

127 Red Fort, Delhi. A procession leaving the Lahore Gate, c. 1830. By an unknown Delhi artist. *India Office Library, London,* ADD.OR.332 (10 × 17 cm.)

128 A harem-carriage of Bahadur Shah II, last Mughul Emperor of Delhi, c. 1848. *India Office Library, London.*

elderly surviving grandson of Jahandar Shah (Farrukhsiyar's short-lived predecessor) who had spent forty years in virtual captivity and had no more capacity than the man he replaced. The new emperor assumed the name of Alamgir, a title which had belonged to Aurangzeb, but he resembled his ancestor in nothing except his simple piety. Yet even this harmless *roi fainéant* managed to arouse Ghazi al-Din's suspicions and in 1759 the *vazir* had him put to death. Ghazi al-Din was still master of Delhi in 1761 when Ahmad Shah Durrani re-entered the city after his victory over the Marathas at Panipat.

Conditions in Delhi in the decades following Nadir Shah's massacre were not conducive to large-scale building operations either by the imperial family or the nobility, nor was there much surplus revenue available. The architecture of mid-eighteenth-century Delhi, if not particularly distinguished, possesses a blowzy stylishness not inappropriate to the spirit of the age. The techniques are unmistakably those inherited from the great builders of a century before and the materials used (mainly red sandstone and white marble) are also the same but the ethereal repose which characterizes the best Islamic building is wholly lacking and the latter-day Mughul dome is almost as onion-shaped as that of a Muscovite church. Fortunately, several examples of this 'Mughul Baroque' have survived subsequent upheavals: the western gateway and mosque in the Qudsiya-Bagh, the Sunahri Masjid (1751) built by the infamous eunuch Javid Khan close to the Delhi Gate of the Fort, and the two tombs at the entrance of the New Delhi Golf Club known as Lal-Bangla, one of which is reputed to contain the graves of Shah Alam's mother and one of his daughters. On a far more ambitious scale is the tomb built by Shuja al-Dowleh for his father, Safdar Jang, shortly after the latter's death in 1754 (cf. fig. 21, page 149). The most recent of the Mughul garden-tombs to have survived up to the twentieth century and having as its prototype the tomb of Humayun, this is a massive square structure dominated by a large, somewhat bulbous dome. It stands on a platform in the centre of a fine walled garden of the *chahar-bagh* type, which is entered by an imposing gateway. In addition to the tomb itself and near the entrance is an elegant little mosque and living quarters for the family's dependants. Much criticized on aesthetic grounds as exemplifying the full decadence of the late Mughul style (Bishop Heber in the early nineteenth century described it somewhat unflatteringly as 'too much of the colour of potted meat'), Safdar Jang's tomb is not without its merits. There are several excellently proportioned rooms, including the octagonal tomb-chamber itself; much of the detail indicates a surprisingly high standard of workmanship in a period when conditions must have been far from easy for artisans and craftsmen; and the material used is, for the most part, of the finest quality – having been plundered from the tomb of the Khan-i Khanan in Nizamuddin.

That a building of such a size, demanding heavy expenditure and concentrated effort in assembling craftsmen and materials, could be commissioned in this turbulent period is a salutary reminder that eighteenth-century Delhi was not quite such a cultural desert as has sometimes been suggested by some of the older historians, and especially by those who sought to demonstrate the value of the *Pax Britannica* by stressing the lawlessness of the preceding age. Notwithstanding murder and mutilation and the dreadful events of 1739 and 1757 the arts continued to flourish. Men of letters were still writing fine Persian and finer Urdu and the books which they produced were often beautiful objects in themselves while the level of craftsmanship displayed in the jewelry and in objects of jade and crystal (of. pls. 100, 101, 102, 103, 105) made for the ruling class fell little below that of the preceding century. Moreover, for the ordinary citizen of Delhi in those years the

Fig. 20 Woman braiding her hair after bathing. Painting from the third quarter of the 18th century. *Johnson 13.6, India Office Library, London.*

dominant personality was neither a puppet-ruler nor a bloodthirsty minister but a scholar and a saint, Shah Waliullah. Born in 1703, the son of a jurist who worked on Aurangzeb's great compilation, the *Fatwa-i Alamgiri*, Shah Waliullah's sanctity was such that even emperors paid him homage and there is no doubt that his appeal to the contemporary Muslim rulers urging them to withstand the Maratha advance into the north was a contributory factor in bringing together the forces which destroyed the Maratha confederacy at Panipat. Among humbler folk he enjoyed a reputation comparable to that of the Chishti saints of five centuries before. If, therefore, eighteenth-century Delhi evokes in the imagination a picture of Muhammad Shah amid a court of buffoons and pimps or Ghazi al-Din flanked by his executioners, the full spectrum must also include Shah Waliullah, devoting all his energy to the renewal of the spiritual life of his community and to narrowing the gulf which had for so long divided mysticism from orthodoxy.

Fig. 21　Safdar Jang's tomb, Delhi. This enormous mausoleum for the second Nawab-Vazir of Oudh was built shortly after his death in 1754 by his son, Shuja Al-Dowleh. Painting by an unknown Delhi artist. *Add. Or. 1809, India Office Library, London.*

1761–1858

The final phase of Mughul rule in Delhi extended for nearly a century, from 1761 to the British siege and sack of 1857, and during the greater part of that time the fate of the city was in the hands of strangers, first the Marathas and then the British, with Lord Lake's campaign of 1803 dividing the period of Maratha from that of British domination.

In 1761 Delhi was without an emperor, the actual incumbent of the throne, Shah Alam, being a refugee in Allahabad. The events of Shah Alam's early years epitomized the insecurity which had haunted Delhi throughout the middle decades of the century. Born in the reign of Muhammad Shah he had witnessed first the sack of Nadir Shah and then that of Ahmad Shah Durrani, when it must have seemed almost inevitable that an Afghan *raj* would replace the nerveless Mughul regime, as in the days of Sher Shah. He had seen his father, Alamgir II, raised to the throne in 1754 by Ghazi al-Din Imad al-Mulk and he had seen the degradation to which the monarchy had been reduced by that awesome protector. He himself had first made a mark upon the political scene in 1758 when he had fled from the Red Fort in fear of his life – a course fully justified by Ghazi al-Din's murder of the emperor in the following year – and sought the protection of the Nawab-Vazir of Oudh, Shuja al-Dowleh (1754–75), the son and successor of Safdar Jang. At that juncture, however, Shuja al-Dowleh could do nothing for him so that although Shah Alam promptly proclaimed himself emperor when the news of his father's murder reached him he dared not try his hand against Ghazi al-Din, now firmly established in Delhi. Then came Panipat and in its wake Ahmad Shah Durrani sought to impose some sort of a settlement upon what remained of the empire in conjunction with Ghazi al-Din and Najib al-Dowleh, an Afghan chieftain from Rohilkhand who was to become the dominant figure on the Delhi scene between 1761 and 1768.

Ahmad Shah Durrani marched out of Delhi for the last time in March 1761 and in a brilliantly executed *coup* shortly afterwards Najib al-Dowleh ousted Ghazi al-Din and took his place as *de facto* ruler of Delhi. From then until 1768, when he withdrew to his headquarters at Najibabad in Bijnor District, he controlled both the imperial city and all the surrounding countryside with the help of his Rohilla Afghan troops, his authority resting upon the title of *mukhtar* (deputy) bestowed on him by Shah Alam who, nevertheless, did not trust him sufficiently to risk returning to his own capital.

The retirement of Najib al-Dowleh left Delhi without a protector again and at the mercy of any adventurer possessing sufficient strength to seize it. Ten years had now passed since Shah Alam had fled from the clutches of Ghazi al-Din and, protected in Allahabad by Shuja al-Dowleh and the East India Company which paid him an annual pension of twenty-six lakhs of rupees, he was far from being uncomfortable in his self-imposed exile. But he was also well aware that, should a local chieftain in the Delhi countryside have ambitions to emulate the career of Najib al-Dowleh, there would be several pliant princelings immured within the Red Fort who could be raised to the throne in his place. With this danger in mind, and notwithstanding the disapproval of the English, he came to terms with the Marathas who occupied the city in his name in return for an immense sum in cash, a promise of the districts of Kora and Allahabad, and revenue assignments worth an additional fifteen lakhs. On these terms Shah Alam entered Delhi as emperor for the first time in January 1772.

The man who had clung to the imperial title so tenaciously in such unfavourable conditions was no mere cipher. Shah Alam was intelligent, versatile and highly cultured, dignified and affable in his manners. Never a commanding personality, however, he had become set in his ways by 1772 while the years as a pensioner in Allahabad had made him indolent and self-indulgent. He was therefore fortunate to have at hand a minister of outstanding ability in the person of Mirza Najaf Khan Zulfiqar al-Dowleh, the last truly effective figure in the history of Mughul Delhi.

Fig. 22 Gold *mohur* of Shah Alam, minted at Shajahanabad, A.H. 1219 (A.D. 1804–5). *British Museum, London. (Actual size)*

Like so many Mughul statesmen, Mirza Najaf Khan was a Persian, a Safavid exile who had fled from Iran in the time of Nadir Shah and who had been in the service of Shuja al-Dowleh and also Mir Kasim, Nawab of Bengal, before joining the imperial party. By a combination of military skill and shrewd diplomacy he managed to preserve the semblance of a kingdom for his master. He reduced the Sikh pressure from the north-west, defeated the Jats of Bharatpur and recovered Agra in 1773, and a year later joined Shuja al-Dowleh against the Rohillas. As a result of all this activity the imperial title once more enjoyed a prestige such as it had not possessed since Nadir Shah's invasion and there can be little doubt that these ten years of Mirza Najaf Khan's ministry, ending abruptly with his death in 1782, were happy ones for Delhi. Both in the city itself and in the surrounding countryside there was comparative tranquillity and both commerce and agriculture began to revive after the misery of the previous decades. The court too sprang to life again and while Shah Alam, although lacking the means for excessive indulgence, diverted himself with clever and amusing people, his great minister watched over the safety of the state. It is unfortunate that no monuments have survived in Delhi to commemorate this pleasant period and that the tomb of Mirza Najaf Khan, located not far from that of Safdar Jang, has now almost completely disappeared.

Following Mirza Najaf Khan's death in 1782 the emperor's position rapidly deteriorated and a powerful protector became more essential than ever. Having failed to enlist the interest of Warren Hastings, Shah Alam turned to the great Maratha chieftain, Madho Rao Sindhia. In 1784 he appointed the infant Peshwa (the head of the Maratha confederacy) as his *vakil-i mutlaq* (Sole Regent) and Sindhia as the Peshwa's deputy. In the countryside around Delhi Sindhia was represented by his Savoyard general, Benoit de Boigne, who established his headquarters at Aligarh and came near to converting the Duab into a French principality.

But before this new regime could be firmly established tragedy struck the emperor. In 1788 Delhi and the Red Fort were unexpectedly seized by Ghulam Qadir, a grandson of Najib al-Dowleh, who plundered the palace, dug up the paving stones and wrenched the marble-facings off the walls in a savage quest for treasure and, having failed to discover any after ten days of wanton vandalism, finally had the emperor blinded. Nothing was left behind in the palace which could be taken away and the surviving inhabitants of the Fort were left without food or a change of clothes. Ghulam Qadir then abandoned Delhi and fled into

151

the Duab where he was defeated in battle near Meerut by de Boigne, captured and executed.

Physical mutilation, which is a disqualification for the exercise of kingship in Islam, should have debarred Shah Alam from retaining his throne, but Sindhia wanted no change. The prestige commanded by Shah Alam after thirty years as emperor was reflected also in Sindhia, his protector, and, in any case, there was no obvious alternative. Moreover Shah Alam himself, according to Warren Hastings' agent, was 'as tenacious of royalty as if it was attended with all the power and renown of Acbar and Aurangzeb'. He was now, more than ever before, a Maratha pensióner but he remained uncommonly sprightly, considering that he was in his seventies and totally blind. His immediate protector, de Boigne, was a humane person and the latter's French-officered brigades kept a rough-and-ready sort of peace in the neighbourhood of the city. Years later, when the French had disappeared from northern India, an inquisitive traveller made enquiries as to what kind of reputation they had left behind and was told that they had been

'often oppressive and avaricious, but as of more conciliating and popular manners than the English Sahibs. Many of them . . . had completely adopted the Indian dress and customs, and most of them were free from that exclusive and intolerant spirit, which makes the English, wherever they go, a caste by themselves, disliking and disliked by all their neighbours.'[18]

A change of masters for both the emperor and his capital came in 1803 when, in the course of the Second Maratha War, Lord Lake advanced on the city after his brilliant engagement at Aligarh. Marching north up the east bank of the Jumna he learnt on 11 September 1803 that on the previous night the general commanding the Maratha forces in Delhi, Louis Bourquin, had crossed the Jumna and that both armies were now advancing towards each other. The exact site of the battle of Delhi cannot be located with any degree of certainty but it was about six miles south of the city and it must have been possible for watchers on the platform of Humayun's tomb to have seen the smoke of the guns beyond the river. It was a bitterly-fought engagement and it was won at the point of the bayonet. Lake himself twice had his horse shot from under him as he exposed himself in the thick of the fighting. When the Marathas withdrew he ordered an immediate advance towards Delhi and the British camp was pitched on the east bank of the Jumna opposite the Old City. Shah Alam hurriedly came to terms with his new conqueror and sent the heir-apparent into the British camp to conduct the Commander-in-Chief to his presence, the two together leading a glittering procession into the city, where an immense crowd of spectators watched them slowly thread their way through the streets. In the Red Fort the emperor, blind, shabbily-dressed and seated under a tattered canopy in the Diwan-i Khass, received his conqueror with a dignity and courtesy which would have done credit to Shah Jahan and, although it was no longer in his power to bestow jewels or elephants, he loaded Lake with sonorous titles:

'Sword of the State, Hero of the land,
Lord of the Age, Victorious in war'.

A courtly soldier who respected the monarchical principle wherever he met it, Lake was honoured by his Mughul titles – as the emperor intended him to be – and he treated Shah Alam with appropriate deference.

Lake did not linger in Delhi but before he set out for Agra, where a powerful Maratha garrison still held the fort, he made arrangements for the administration

Fig. 23 Lieutenant-Colonel James Skinner, C.B. (1778–1841), the founder of Skinner's Horse and one of the most colourful figures in early 19th-century Delhi. *Collection of Mrs Basil Wood Bourne.*

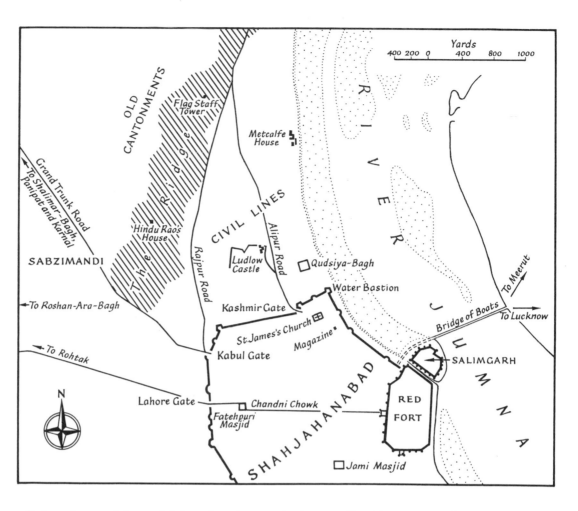

Old Delhi (northern section) and the Civil Lines, 1857.

of the city and its neighbourhood, appointing as Resident at the Mughul court Colonel David Ochterlony under whose genial supervision – despite a sudden scare when Holkar's Marathas made a dash for the city in October 1804, necessitating a hurried restoration of Shah Jahan's crumbling walls – Delhi entered the somnolent Residency period, that picturesque twilight of the imperial city made familiar by the work of the Daniells, and other English artists, as well as from the pages of contemporary diaries and letters.

Inside the Red Fort, Shah Alam and his two successors continued to rule over their relatives and dependants for more than half a century, maintaining as far as their slender means allowed the traditions of times past. The coinage was still minted in the emperor's name and his name continued to be read out in the *khutba* every Friday, but no sentence of death or mutilation could be carried out without the Resident's assent and the substance of power now emanated from the imposing Residency compound on the northern side of the Old City, beyond which a typical nineteenth-century British-Indian suburb, the Civil Lines, grew up between the Qudsiya-Bagh and the Ridge (cf. map above).

The first Resident, Ochterlony, maintained the sumptuous standards of the old Mughul nobility (cf. pl. 120) and passed the uncomfortable summer months in almost royal state in the old Shalimar-Bagh off the Karnal Road, where Aurangzeb had been crowned and Nadir Shah had rested before entering the city as a conqueror. Ochterlony's Delhi abounded in colourful figures but two stood head and shoulders above the rest. The first was the Anglo-Indian soldier of fortune, Colonel James Skinner (cf. fig. 23, page 152), an inspired leader of irregular cavalry

153

who made Skinner's Horse one of the most distinguished as well as one of the most colourful bodies of men in the Company's army. Skinner's memorial in Delhi is St James's Church (cf. fig. 25, page 159), built in fulfilment of a vow made many years before on a Maratha battlefield, and inside the church a plaque and his favourite pew survived the upheaval of the Mutiny, as did his town-house across the street.

The other outstanding figure in early nineteenth-century Delhi was the Begum Samru, a Kashmiri dancing-girl who married the German adventurer, Walther Reinhard (usually known as Sombre), turned Christian and, during a long widowhood prior to her death in 1836, ruled with vigour the *jagir* of Sardhana, near Meerut, first as an ally of the emperor, then of the Marathas, and finally of the British. Like Skinner's house, the Begum's palace off Chandni-Chowk escaped serious damage in the Mutiny but the building which most fitly commemorates the career of this remarkable woman is the enormous Roman Catholic basilica at Sardhana which houses her handsome white-marble cenotaph brought all the way from Rome where it was carved.

Shah Alam died in 1806 and was succeeded by his son, Akbar Shah (cf. pl. 120), a colourless personality whose reception of Bishop Heber in 1824 inspired an account of the occasion which reveals the utter decay which had overtaken the Mughul court. Heber went to the Red Fort accompanied by the Resident (H. M. Elliott) and a procession of elephants, entering by the Lahore Gate where the bodyguard was drawn up inside Aurangzeb's barbican. Continuing their way on elephants through 'the noblest gateway and vestibule which I ever saw' and through the long covered passage (Chhatta-Chowk), which Heber likened to a cathedral aisle, they came to a 'ruinous and exceedingly dirty stable-yard'. Here they were met by functionaries with large gold-headed canes and they dismounted. The bishop then proceeded towards the Naqqar-Khana surrounded by a swarm of beggars and making slow progress in his cassock and gown while his thin shoes squelched through the mud left by a recent shower of rain.

'After this we passed another richly-carved, but ruinous and dirty gateway, where our guides, withdrawing a canvas screen, called out, in a sort of harsh chaunt, "Lo, the ornament of the world! Lo, the asylum of the nations! King of Kings! The Emperor Acbar Shah! Just, fortunate, victorious!" We saw, in fact, a large handsome and striking court, about as big as that at All Souls, with low, but richly-ornamented buildings. Opposite to us was a beautiful open pavilion of white marble, richly carved, flanked by rose-bushes and fountains, and some tapestry and striped curtains hanging in festoons about it, within which was a crowd of people and the poor old descendant of Tamerlane seated in the midst of them. Mr Elliott here bowed three times very low, in which we followed his example. The ceremony was repeated twice as we advanced up the steps of the pavilion, the heralds each time repeating the same expressions about their master's greatness. We then stood in a row on the right-hand side of the throne, which is a sort of marble bedstead richly ornamented with gilding, and raised on two or three steps.'[19]

Then followed the traditional exchange of gifts, the presentation to the emperor of *nazars* of gold *mohurs*, the customary expressions of civility and the donning of *khilats*. To remove the latter, Heber withdrew to a nearby room where he had time to observe his surroundings in detail.

'While in the small apartment where I got rid of my shining garments, I was struck by its beautiful ornaments. It was entirely lined with white marble, inlaid with flowers and leaves of green serpentine, lapis lazuli, and blue and red porphyry; the flowers were of the best Italian style of workmanship, and evidently the labour of an artist of that country. All, however, was dirty, desolate, and forlorn. Half the flowers and leaves had been picked out or otherwise defaced, and the doors and windows were in a state of dilapidation, while a quantity of old furniture was piled in one corner, and a torn hanging of tapestry hung over an archway which led to the interior apartments.'[20]

On emerging from this room he was informed that the emperor had withdrawn into the harem and he was thus able to examine carefully the workmanship in the Diwan-i Khass and walk in the once-magnificent gardens, now depressingly forlorn, with their dried-up watercourses and the evidence of neglect everywhere. Strolling in the Hayat-Baksh-Bagh (cf. pls. 113, 117) he particularly admired the octagonal pavilion on the north-eastern corner of the walls with a fountain in its centre and a beautiful bath in a recess. This too, however, he found 'dirty, lonely, and wretched; the bath and fountain dry; the inlaid pavement hid with lumber and gardener's sweepings, and the walls stained with the dung of birds and bats'. He found Aurangzeb's mosque and the Diwan-i Am in the same neglected condition, and with the throne in the latter 'so covered with pigeon's dung, that its ornaments were hardly discernible'.

Of the emperor himself, Heber was equally observant:

'He has a pale, thin, but handsome face, with an aquiline nose, and a long white beard. His complexion is little if at all darker than that of a European. His hands are very fair and delicate, and he had some valuable-looking rings on them. His hands and face were all I saw of him, for the morning being cold, he was so wrapped up in shawls, that he reminded me extremely of the Druid's head on a Welch halfpenny . . . Acbar Shah has the appearance of a man of seventy-four or seventy-five; he is, however, not much turned of sixty-three, but, in this country, that is a great age. He is said to be a very good-tempered, mild, old man, of moderate talents, but polished and pleasing manners. His favourite wife, the Begum, is a low-born, low-bred, and violent woman, who rules him completely, lays hold on all his money, and has often influenced him to very unwise conduct towards his children, and the British Government. She hates her eldest son [the future Emperor Bahadur Shah II], who is, however, a respectable man, of more talents than native princes usually shew, and, happily for himself, has a predilection for those literary pursuits which are almost the only laudable or innocent objects of ambition in his power. He is fond of poetry, and is himself a very tolerable Persian poet. He has taken some pains with the education of his children, and, what in this country is very unusual, even of his daughters.'[21]

During his stay in Delhi Heber was shrewd enough to appreciate that over the past twenty years relations between the Mughuls and the British had deteriorated. The first British Residents in Delhi after Lord Lake had been meticulous in paying the respect that was due to the emperor. But now the Englishmen who served the Company belonged to a new generation which scoffed at the harmless ceremonies performed in the emperor's presence and deplored the waste of the twelve or fifteen lakhs of rupees which made up his annual pension. As the first quarter of the nineteenth century drew to its close few Englishmen had the magnanimity or the political acumen of Sir John Malcolm, who wrote of the Delhi regime:

'If the King of Delhi was in fact an absurdity or a mockery (I do not admit it was either), it had its root in a wise conformance to usage, in a generous consideration of the feelings of fallen greatness. It was the veneration of a great power that had passed away . . .'[22]

But Malcolm's was almost a lone voice in an age when Evangelical and Utilitarian ideals were spreading rapidly among the Company's servants and from which Delhi was only partially sheltered by the long occupation of the Residency by the

Metcalfes. Sir Charles Metcalfe was Resident from 1811 to 1819, and again from 1825 to 1827, and – like Ochterlony – he used the Shalimar-Bagh as a summer residence where he kept his Sikh wife and children. His brother, Thomas Theophilus, lived in Delhi between 1813 and 1853 and was responsible for the building of Metcalfe House, a large mansion on the banks of the Jumna north of Old Delhi, which he filled with a magnificent library, fashionable French furniture and a collection of Napoleonic relics. For a summer retreat he preferred Mehrauli to the Shalimar-Bagh and there he converted the octagonal tomb of Muhammad Quli Khan (a brother of Adham Khan, Akbar's foster-brother) near the Qutb-Minar into a charming country residence known as Dilgusha ('Heart's Delight'). William Fraser, Governor-General's Agent until his assassination in 1835, preferred the Ridge and occupied a large building later celebrated during the Mutiny as Hindu Rao's House and now the site of the Hindu Rao Hospital.

Meanwhile Delhi itself was enjoying a profound peace stretching back from 1857 to the *emeute* of Ghulam Qadir seventy years before. Most of the inhabitants still lived within Shah Jahan's walls but, north of the Kashmir Gate, an English suburb had grown up beneath the Ridge while to the south the tombs and other monuments in Nizamuddin and around the Qutb-Minar sheltered not only peaceful villagers but also ruffians and *badmashas*. Compared to the metropolis it had been in the reign of Shah Jahan, Delhi was now a relatively small city but it was also a prosperous one. The price of food was low and the population was beginning to expand again. For the poor life was no doubt hard – it always had been – but for the upper and middling classes it was a comfortable, indolent existence not very different from that of *nawabi* Lucknow as described by Mirza Muhammad Rusva in his *Umrao Jan Ada*. Within the Fort, too, life continued its unchanging routine notwithstanding the fact that in 1837 Akbar Shah died and was succeeded by his son, Bahadur Shah II (cf. pl. 99). The place of this last of the Mughuls in the life of the city has been imaginatively described by Percival Spear and his account – part of which is quoted below – can scarcely be bettered:

'Bahadur Shah was educated to the life of a mediatized prince, and the role fitted him perfectly. Whether he could have developed the qualities of action we shall never know, for he was denied all opportunity in his early years and the Mutiny experience came far too late. But as a philosophic prince he would have adorned any court. He would have made a dignified ruler of a minor German state under the Empire or an excellent constitutional king. Delhi in his time was an Indian Weimar, with Ghalib for its Goethe. His interests and tastes were primarily literary and aesthetic. He loved poetry and philosophy, gardens and nature in all its guises. Nearly every day of his life he went for excursions across the Jumna morning and evening; every monsoon found him established at Mehrauli, where he built himself a country palace . . . He enjoyed gardens and laid out at least two himself, one below the palace wall on the Jumna bank and one at Shahdara. He loved animals and had a special fondness for doves. He was religious without being fanatical, and learned without being pedantic . . .

But above all Bahadur Shah was a poet and a literary patron. He was the pupil and friend of Zauq, whose rival was the famous Ghalib. He composed several volumes of lyrics, some of which attained considerable popularity. Though not quite in the same rank as Ghalib or Zauq he has his niche in the Urdu pantheon and his merit cannot be denied. It is this gift, much more than his crown, which gave him his place in the life of Delhi, and it is this even more than his political misfortunes, which has caused him to be affectionately remembered by the people.'[23]

Much of his time, however, was occupied with the disputes of his relatives since, in addition to his own wives and children, the children and grandchildren of Akbar

Fig. 24 Silver rupee of Bahadur Shah II, minted at Shajahanabad, A.H. 1254 (A.D. 1838–9). *British Museum, London. (Actual size)*

Shah and even of Shah Alam, the Fort still contained numerous descendants of Shah Jahan and his successors, known collectively as the *salatin*. Living in acute destitution and virtual captivity, these numbered 2,104 in 1848. Their future, however, was a bleak one for Bahadur Shah was aging and it was widely believed that on his death no successor would be recognized and the dynasty would become extinct. And then the quiet routine of the palace, which had hardly changed for half a century or more, was rudely shattered. On the morning of 11th May 1857 the sepoys, who had mutinied at Meerut and had marched hot-foot to Delhi, entered the southern part of the city. Before the day was over they had been admitted to the Fort, the Magazine (the gateways of which still stand in front of the General Post Office) had been blown up after a desperate resistance by a handful of British soldiers and the European community had either been killed, had fled into the Fort for protection or had made their way to the Flagstaff Tower on the Ridge, which they left at dusk, straggling up the Grand Trunk Road to the safety of the cantonments at Ambala (cf. map page 153). That same day, a party of mutineers had forced their way into the presence of Bahadur Shah, had seated him upon his throne and had paid homage to him – although with scant signs of respect.

Predictably, the Fort became the rallying point for the mutineers in Delhi and the Mughul princes came to the fore as honorary commanders of the troops. With the growing spirit of violence, a demand arose for the death of the fifty European women and children who had fled into the Fort and who were now closely-guarded prisoners. Bahadur Shah's ministers opposed this action, both on grounds of humanity and expediency, but they were denounced as traitors for their luke-warmness to the cause and on the 16th of May a rabble of soldiers surrounded the Diwan-i Khass, while inside Bahadur Shah and his ministers were besieged by those demanding the death-sentence. What happened at the meeting was never revealed but eventually one of the princes, Mirza Mughul, left the hall declaring that permission for the execution had been given. The prisoners were then dragged out in front of the Naqqar-Khana, the scene of more than one royal murder, and there butchered.

Within the city itself the greatest danger came from the risk of communal outbreaks but these were successfully averted – largely through the personal inter-vention of the king. There were, however, other sources of trouble. The new regime badly needed funds and as there was little in the way of legitimate revenue the troops soon resorted to extortion, especially of the commercial and banking classes. The princes also took to extortion on their own account against a background of mounting disorder, indiscipline, looting and accusations of treason which in turn served as a justification for further violence and plundering. Then the siege began.

By the 8th of June a British army was entrenched on the Ridge north-west of the city, the men suffering incredible agony from the heat and largely immobile on account of their small numbers. Delhi itself was far from beleaguered. The road to Muttra was open for a number of weeks, supplies continued to be brought up river by barge, and the bridge-of-boats across the Jumna remained open. Once the British were established on the Ridge, however, their camp offered an attractive market where villagers from the surrounding countryside could dispose of their grain, and the price of food soared in the city accordingly.

For weeks neither side could gain any advantage but in early September a change came when John Nicholson led the long-awaited siege-train from the Panjab into the British camp. It was only a matter of days before the heavy batteries, without which the besiegers could make no impression on the massive walls, were in position and on the 14th of September came the assault and Nicholson's death at the Kashmir Gate. There followed several days of confused fighting until all further resistance had been eliminated. Then came, as the climax to the months of suffering for the people of Delhi, the horrors of a full-scale sack by troops driven to the limits of their endurance by a summer on the Ridge. The unsystematic looting of the first units to enter the city was, however, soon replaced by the methodical pillaging of the Prize Agents, while the surviving population was driven out into the surrounding countryside to starve or survive as best they could. As late as December many were still living without shelter outside the walls, mainly around the Qutb-Minar and in Nizamuddin. The city itself was deserted. 'For miles not a creature save a half-starved cat,' wrote one visitor, 'and here and there an old hag groping about amidst the bones, old papers, and rags with which this once wealthy and populous place is strewed. It is as a city of the dead.'

As soon as it became known that the British had gained a foothold in the city, Bahadur Shah and his family fled from the Fort to the gardens surrounding Humayun's tomb, accompanied by a number of troops who sheltered in the nearby Arab-Sarai. Further resistance, however, was out of the question and negotiations were begun for the surrender of the imperial family. On receipt of a safe-conduct from the British commander, Bahadur Shah, accompanied by his queen and his favourite son, Jivan Bakht, returned to the Fort where he remained for over a year, confined to cramped, uncomfortable quarters and exposed to the humiliating gaze of idle sightseers. A military commission was set up to investigate his role in the recent uprising. As a result of its findings, based on evidence which bears little scrutiny today, the old emperor was sent into perpetual exile in Rangoon, accompanied by his queen, some members of his former household, mainly women, and by Jivan Bakht. Descendants of the latter are said to have been still residing there within living memory.

One last incident remains to be told. When Bahadur Shah surrendered to Captain Hodgson the Mughul princes who had accompanied him in his flight from the Red Fort lingered at Humayun's tomb, uncertain of what to do next. There three of them (two sons and a grandson) were later arrested by Hodgson and taken back to Delhi on a bullock-cart. Not far from the southern limits of the Old City he turned them out of the cart, ordered them to strip, and then pistolled them – subsequently justifying his action on the grounds that an attempt might have been made by their followers to rescue them. Tradition locates the murders at the solitary Kabul Gate of Sher Shah's city, which has since acquired the nickname of the Khuni-Darwaza, the Gate of Blood. The corpses were then taken back to Humayun's tomb and there, in the building which, more than any other, commemorates the final establishment of Mughul rule in India and where a score of luckless candidates for the Peacock Throne received anonymous burial, the sons of Bahadur Shah were interred – and with them the story of Mughul Delhi.

The suppression of the Mutiny brought to a sudden, unequivocal close the story of Mughul rule in India, a transformation felt more severely in Delhi than perhaps anywhere else. For more than two centuries Fatehpur Sikri had been a picturesque ruin while from the time when Lord Lake occupied Agra in 1803 the latter city had been a quiet backwater, a divisional headquarters and a nest of English provincial society. Lahore, where so much of the splendour and drama of Mughul India had been enacted, had become the capital of the model British province of the Panjab in 1849 and prior to that had been for half a century the capital of an infidel Sikh *raj*. Hyderabad, it is true, was to retain vestiges of its Mughul past up to 1947 but wanton Lucknow had passed into British hands a year before the Mutiny when Lord Dalhousie had proclaimed the annexation of Oudh and had sent its pleasure-loving, scapegrace ruling dynasty packing. All these cities had felt in varying degrees the gradual spread of British power and influence across the country (Hyderabad perhaps less than the others) but for Delhi the impact when it came had been more cataclysmic, because of the destruction caused during the 1857 outbreak, and more decisive because of the absolute break with the past which followed it.

It was, of course, inevitable that the disappearance of the court and the establishment of a new regime would bring about profound changes in the appearance of the city as well as in the lives of its citizens; the wonder is that so few of the radical reprisals advocated by vengeful hot-heads found official support –

Fig. 25   St James's Church, Delhi, c. 1858. This drawing was made just after the damage which the building sustained during the Mutiny had been repaired. *Mss Eur D. 512/1 fo. 37v. India Office Library, London.*

159

a measure of the good sense of Sir John Lawrence, then Chief Commissioner of the Panjab. The climate of English opinion in the period immediately following the Mutiny can, however, be judged by a proposal from the city magistrate, Philip Egerton, that the Jami Masjid 'be used as a Christian Church, and on each of the thousand compartments of the marble floor, the name of one of our Christian martyrs be inscribed'. It had already served as a Sikh barracks.

The Red Fort was turned over to the military authorities to house a British garrison. Buildings which were not deemed to be of outstanding architectural importance by the standards of a not very discriminating age were demolished and their place taken by the hideous barracks which still stand, their gaping windows overlooking what was once the inner sanctum of the palace. It is surely time that these and other monstrosities within the Fort were pulled down and the space vacated laid out as gardens. In front of the Fort an extensive area in what had once been the heart of the old city was cleared of houses in order to increase the security of the garrison, resulting in the destruction of a vast amount of property for which compensation appears to have been not altogether adequate. The extent of this operation is still clearly visible today. At the same time, tangible reminders of the events of 1857 were carefully preserved. Within the city itself St James's Church, damaged during the siege, was restored (cf. fig. 25, page 159) and the gateways to the former Magazine left as they had been after the explosion on the afternoon of the 11th of May. On the Ridge a Gothic memorial was raised to the fallen British and their allies on the site of the siege-battery which covered the extreme right wing of the besieging force, and close to the Kashmir Gate a garden was laid out in which a statue of John Nicholson was erected by public subscription.

Between 1858 and 1947 Delhi experienced almost ninety years of comparative tranquillity under the aegis of the *Pax Britannica*. As the nineteenth century wore on, the Public Works Department steadily wrought its unimaginative will upon the face of the city: macadamized roads thrust their way through crumbling gateways and barbicans and jerry-built offices and godowns smothered the ramparts. The East India Railway breached the walls beside Salimgarh, and the Delhi, Umballa and Kalka Railway, opened in 1891, close to the Kabul Gate. The English were now living in Delhi in greater numbers than ever before and with less discomfort than in pre-Mutiny days, although it is surprising to read that in 1859 a young official down from the Panjab for his wedding could not find a clergyman in Delhi to perform the service and had to ride first to Bulandshahr and then to the Bengal Artillery Mess at Meerut before he could locate a padre.

But if they were more numerous than in the days when the Metcalfes ruled from the Residency, the English of post-Mutiny Delhi were also less colourful and more conventional, the parochial routine of their lives contrasting strangely with the half-forgotten splendour of their surroundings. On a visit in 1876 Alfred Lyall, one of the more imaginative proconsuls of his generation, sensed something of the incongruity.

Hardly a shot from the gate we stormed,
Under the Moree battlement's shade;
Close to the glacis our game was formed,
There had the fight been, and there we played.

Lightly the demoiselles tittered and leapt,
Merrily capered the players all;
North, was the garden where Nicholson slept,
South, was the sweep of a battered wall.

Near me a Musalman, civil and mild,
Watched as the shuttlecocks rose and fell;
And he said, as he counted his beads and smiled,
'God smite their souls to the depths of hell'.

A year later Delhi was selected by Lord Lytton as the setting for the brilliant Durbar at which Queen Victoria was proclaimed *Kaisar-i Hind* ('Empress of India') and in the first flush of his enthusiasm he assured the Queen that 'those who saw it will probably never again behold in one spot so vivid and various a display of strange arms, strange uniforms, and strange figures . . .' In this, however, he was wrong, for within less than thirty years Lord Curzon, to whom more than to anyone else is due the preservation of the monuments of Delhi and Agra, celebrated the accession of King Edward VII with even greater magnificence. It was at the last of these glittering assemblies, held in 1911, that King George V announced that Delhi would replace Calcutta as the capital of the Indian Empire. From that decision stemmed the foundation of an eighth city around the spacious nucleus designed by Sir Edwin Lutyens and Sir Herbert Baker which is today the capital of an independent India.

Ninety years of British rule and twenty more of independence have altered the city's features almost beyond recognition and, although Delhi is now a rapidly expanding metropolis, it requires very considerable imagination to visualize what it must have been like in the days of Firuz Shah Tughluq or Shah Jahan, when it was the heart of a great Islamic empire and a centre of Islamic culture and learning comparable to medieval Baghdad or Samarqand. Unlike Safavid Isfahan where past and present rub shoulders on easy terms, the ghosts of Mughul Delhi have been well laid and it is hard to realize that in the narrow streets behind the Jami Masjid there are perhaps old men still living whose grandfathers knew Ghalib or watched the bullock-carriages of the last Mughul emperor lurching across the bridge of boats beyond Salimgarh into a forlorn exile.

Notes

1 H. A. R. Hamilton Gibb, *Ibn Battuta. Travels in Asia and Africa, 1325–1354*, London, 1929, p. 184.   2 A. S. Beveridge, *The Babur-name in English*, 2 vols., London, 1922, vol. 1, p. 283.   3 *Ibid*, vol. 2, pp. 518–520.   4 *Ibid*, vol. 2, p. 532.   5 D. N. Mackenzie, *Poems from the Divan of Khushal Khan Khattak*, London, 1965, p. 93. I have deliberately avoided making a distinction between Afghan and Pathan. The origins of both names are discussed at length in O. Caroe's *The Pathans*, London, 1958.   6 Percival Spear, *A History of India*, vol. 2, London, 1965, p. 26.   7 *Ain-i-Akbari of Abul Fazl-i-Allami*, translated by H. Blochmann, Col. H. S. Jarrett, and Sir Jadunath Sarkar, 3 vols., Calcutta, 1927–1948, vol. 3, p. 451.   8 Reginald Heber, *Narrative of a Journey through the Upper Provinces of India, from Calcutta to Bombay, 1824–1825*, 3 vols., 4th edition, London, 1829, vol. 2, p. 336.   9 Abu Talib Kalim. E. G. Brown, *A Literary History of Persia*, Cambridge, 1959, vol. 4, p. 260.   10 H. Goetz: 'Persia and India after the conquest of Mahmud', in *The Legacy of Persia*, edited by A. J. Arberry, Oxford, 1953, pp. 112–113.   11 H. Goetz, *India. Five Thousand Years of Indian Art*, London, 1959, p. 218.   12 Sir Malcolm Darling, *Apprentice to Power. India, 1904–1908*, London, 1966, p. 136.   13 E. M. Forster, *The Hill of Devi*, London, 1965, p. 124.   14 S. Sen, *Indian Travels of Thevenot and Careri*, New Delhi, 1949, pp. 47–49.   15 N. Manucci, *Storia do Mogor*, translated and edited by W. Irvine, 4 vols., 1907–1908, vol. 1, p. 231.   16 Quoted in Muhammad Sadiq's *A History of Urdu Literature*, London, 1964, p. 60.   17 *Ibid*, p. 100.   18 Reginald Heber, *Ibid*, vol. 2, pp. 343–344.   19 *Ibid*, p. 302.   20 *Ibid*, p. 299.   21 *Ibid*, p. 313.   22 From an undated letter from John Malcolm to Gerald Wellesley quoted in J. W. Kaye: *The Life and Correspondence of Major-General Sir John Malcolm, G.C.B.*, 2 vols., London, 1856, vol. 2, pp. 377–378.   23 Percival Spear, *Twilight of the Mughuls*, Cambridge, 1951, pp. 73–74.

Acknowledgements

The Publishers would like to express their gratitude to all those who assisted Wim Swaan during his visit to India to take most of the photographs reproduced in this volume. They would also like to thank those individuals, museums and libraries which helped by providing photographs of miniatures, drawings, prints and objects in their collections.

The illustrations are acknowledged to the following sources: Reproduced by courtesy of the Trustees of the British Museum, London: plates 1, 51, 97, 118, 121, 122; figures 2, 3, 4, 5, 7, 8, 10, 11, 13, 17, 22, 24. Reproduced by courtesy of the Victoria and Albert Museum, London: plates 19, 20, 21, 22, 23, 24, 25, 47, 61, 62, 63, 64, 65, 75, 76, 77, 78, 79, 80, 81, 89, 94, 95, 98, 100, 101, 102, 103, 104, 105, 106, 107, 108, 109, 110, 111, 119; back of jacket. Chester Beatty Library, Dublin: front of jacket; plates 9, 50. Metropolitan Museum of Art, New York: plates 48, 55, 56, 73; figure 6. Collection of Alice and Nasli Heeramaneck, New York: plates 49, 52. Dr Percival Spear: plate 99. Reproduced by courtesy of the Secretary of State for Commonwealth Affairs, London: plates 120, 123, 124, 125, 126, 127, 128; figures 9, 15, 18, 19, 20, 21, 23, 25. SCR Photo Library, London: figure 1. Bibliothèque Nationale, Paris: figures 12, 16. Calouste Gulbenkian Foundation, Oeiras: figure 14. Reproduced by courtesy of Mrs Basil Wood Bourne: figure 23.

In addition to those photographs taken by Wim Swaan, the Publishers wish to acknowledge that others were taken by J. R. Freeman, London, and Rex Roberts Studios, Dublin, and that the maps were drawn by Gillian Andrew.

The following have kindly given their permission for the reproduction of extracts from books published by them: Methuen & Co. Ltd, London; Crown Publishers Inc., New York; and Holle & Company N.V., The Netherlands, for the extract from H. Goetz: *India. Five Thousand Years of Indian Art;* The National Archives of India, New Delhi, for the extract from S. Sen, *Indian Travels of Thevenot and Careri;* Cambridge University Press for the extract from Percival Spear, *Twilight of the Mughuls;* Oxford University Press, Karachi, for the extract from M. Sadiq, *A History of Urdu Literature;* Edward Arnold Ltd, London, for the extract from E. M. Forster, *The Hill of Devi;* The Clarendon Press, Oxford, for the extract from H. Goetz, 'Persia and India after the Conquest of Mahmud', *The Legacy of Persia*, edited by A. J. Arberry; George Allen and Unwin Ltd, London, for the extract from *The Poems of the Divan of Khushal Khan Khattak*, translated by D. N. MacKenzie.

amir	A military commander; a member of the Mughul ruling class.
arak	An alcoholic beverage popular among the Turks and Persians.
badmash	A ruffian; a bad character.
Chaghatai	(i) The second son of Chingiz Khan, d. 1241; (ii) An inhabitant of the Central Asian Khanate ruled by his descendants; (iii) the Turkish language of that Khanate which the Mughuls brought with them into India.
chahar-bagh	A Persian garden divided into four principal parterres by paths and watercourses.
chhatri	A small kiosk or pavilion constructed on the roof of a building as, for example, on the roof of Humayun's tomb.
Chishti	The *Chishti* dervish-order (*silsila*) was introduced into India by Khwaja Muin al-Din Chishti of Ajmer (1141–1236) and rapidly established a reputation for sanctity. Although supported by successive rulers of Delhi, the *Chishtis* usually refused to embroil themselves in politics which they held to be, by their nature, ungodly.
crore	100 *lakhs* or 10,000,000 rupees, equal in the 19th century to one million pounds sterling. The term is still used extensively in India and carries, naturally enough, the connotation of immense wealth. It was said that, in the early 19th century, the Nawab-Vazir of Oudh had paid out in loans to the East India Company a full crore of rupees for the privilege of being styled 'King of Oudh'.
diwan	(i) A collection of poems; (ii) the title of the principal revenue official of the Mughul Empire; (iii) a hall or chamber used for administration etc., such as the *Diwan-i Am* (the Emperor's Public Audience Hall) and the *Diwan-i Khass* (the Emperor's Private Audience Hall).
Duab	The land lying between two rivers; especially the area between the Jumna and the Ganges.
gardi	A calamity or visitation, such as the sack of a city.
hajj	The pilgrimage to Mecca.
jagir	An assignment of land.
jagirdar	The holder of a *jagir*.
jauhar	The Rajput custom whereby the women and children of a beleaguered garrison immolate themselves, and the men vow not to survive a last engagement.
jizya	A poll-tax levied by a Muslim state upon its non-Muslim subjects.
khan	An honorific title used by the Mughuls in India and originating with the Turko-Mongol tribes of Central Asia.
Khass Mahal	The emperor's private apartments in the forts at Delhi and Agra.

khilat	A robe of honour conferred by a superior.
khutba	The prayers read in the congregational mosque (*Jami Masjid*) on Friday, in which God's support is invoked for the legitimate sovereign.
lakh	100,000 rupees, a term still used extensively in India. The purchasing power of the rupee has fallen steadily over the past three or four centuries. During most of the 19th century the rupee was equivalent to two shillings. W. H. Moreland in his *India at the Death of Akbar* (London, 1920) estimated that the rupee during the reign of Akbar had six times the purchasing power it enjoyed in his own day.
madraseh	A Muslim theological college.
mahal	A house, palace or district.
mansab	An official rank in the Mughul governing hierarchy.
mansabdar	The holder of a *mansab*.
masjid	A mosque.
Mawarannahr	The area in Turkestan between the Amu-Darya and the Syr-Darya. Like the Greek form, i.e. Transoxania, the Arabic *Mawarannahr* means literally 'The Land beyond the River'.
minar	A minaret.
mohur	A gold coin valued at different times between ten and fifteen rupees.
nadirshahi	A calamity or visitation, such as the sack of a city.
nawab	The title of a Mughul prince or governor.
nazar	An offering, usually of money, from an inferior to a superior.
Nuruz	The Persian New Year.
Padshah	The emperor.
palki	A palanquin.
pir	A Muslim saint.
raj	Rule; dominion.
salatin	In nineteenth-century Delhi this word was used to describe the descendants of Shah Jahan who were part-pensioners and part-prisoners in the Red Fort.
sayyid	A descendant of the Prophet Muhammad.
shaykh	A Muslim saint or scholar.
shikari	A hunter.
sijda	The act of prostration.
silsila	A dervish-order, such as that of the *Chishtiyeh*.
subah	A Mughul province.
subahdar	The governor of a *subah*.
Sufi	A Muslim mystic; a dervish.
ulama	Persons learned in the Muslim religious sciences.
vakil	An agent; someone acting on behalf of someone else, as a regent acts on behalf of a king (hence *vakil-i mutlaq*, Sole Regent). In Mughul India the emperor's chief minister.
vazir	In Mughul India the official responsible for the finances of the empire.

There is no lack of material on Muslim rule in northern India but the best introduction is *A History of India* by Romila Thapar and Percival Spear, 2 vols., London, 1965–6. For detailed dynastic history *The Cambridge History of India*, vols. 3 and 4, Cambridge, 1928 and 1937, is still useful. Social and cultural developments are thoughtfully discussed in I. H. Qureshi's *The Muslim Community in the Indo-Pakistani Sub-continent*, The Hague, 1963, and in Aziz Ahmad's *Studies in Islamic Culture in the Indian Environment*, Oxford, 1964, while the intellectual milieu can be sampled in the extracts quoted in *Sources of Indian Tradition*, edited by W. T. de Bary, New York, 1958. For the Sultanate period Peter Hardy's *Historians of Medieval India*, London, 1960, is particularly stimulating.

The earliest Turkish invasions of India are described in Muhammad Nazim's *The Life and Times of Sultan Mahmud of Ghazna*, Cambridge, 1931, which should be supplemented by C. E. Bosworth's *The Ghaznavids*, Edinburgh, 1963. The architectural antecedents of the Qutb-Minar in Ghurid Afghanistan are dealt with in *Le Minaret.de Djam*, by André Maricq and Gaston Wiet, Paris, 1959. For a summary of the Central Asian heritage of the Mughuls, see Gavin Hambly's 'Das Reich des Tschaghatai' and Mahin Hajianpur's 'Das Timuridenreich und die Eroberung von Mawarannahr durch die Usbeken' in *Zentralasien*, edited by Gavin Hambly, Frankfurt, 1966. Babur's memoirs are invaluable for the early Mughul period and the best translation is A. S. Beveridge's *The Babur-nama in English*, 2 vols., London, 1922. A detailed narrative in the grand manner is W. Erskine's *A History of India under the two first Sovereigns of the House of Taimur, Baber and Humayun*, 2 vols., London, 1854.

The best introduction to the elusive personality of Akbar is still Laurence Binyon's charming essay, *Akbar*, London, 1932. V. A. Smith's *Akbar the Great Mogul*, Oxford, 1917, was long considered a definitive biography but its reputation is being steadily eroded by subsequent research. The reigns of his successors are covered by B. Prasad's *History of Jahangir*, Allahabad, 1962; B. P. Saksena's *A History of Shahjahan of Dilhi*, Allahabad, 1962; and Jadunath Sarker's *A Short History of Aurangzib*, London, 1930. A recent work of great importance is M. Athar Ali's *The Mughul Nobility under Aurangzeb*, London, 1966. A mass of information, not always impeccably accurate, concerning daily life in seventeenth-century India is contained in the writings of such European travellers as Roe, Bernier, Thévenot, Tavernier, Careri and Manucci.

For the later Mughuls, whose reigns have been described in the narratives of William Irvine and Jadunath Sarkar, there is one work of outstanding value, Satis Chandra's *Parties and Politics at the Mughal Court, 1707–1740*, Aligarh, 1959. There are detailed studies of the two great scourges of eighteenth-century Delhi: Lawrence Lockhart's *Nadir Shah*, London, 1938, and G. Singh's *Ahmad Shah Durrani*, Bombay, 1959. For Delhi itself in its declining years there is Percival Spear's definitive *Twilight of the Mughuls: Studies in Late Mughul Delhi*, Cambridge,

1951, a wonderfully evocative account of the great city in decay. Among contemporary accounts two of the most picturesque are W. Francklin's *History of the Reign of Shah Aulum*, London, 1798, and J. Baillie Fraser's *Military Memoir of Lieut.-Col. James Skinner, C.B.*, 2 vols., London, 1851. In a wholly different genre the famous Urdu novel *Umrao Jan Ada* by Mirza Muhammad Rusva (translated into English by K. Singh and M. A. Husaini, Calcutta, 1961), describing the lives of the courtesans and swashbucklers who served the pleasures of the pre-Mutiny Oudh aristocracy in the brothels and bazaars of *nawabi* Lucknow, illuminates many facets of social behaviour in late-Mughul Delhi. The literary achievements of the eighteenth and nineteenth centuries are imaginatively discussed in Muhammad Sadiq's *A History of Urdu Literature*, London, 1964.

For the architecture of the Sultanate and Mughul periods the relevant chapters in *The Cambridge History of India* provide admirable introductory essays. Percy Brown's *Indian Architecture (Islamic Period)*, Bombay, 1942, is also useful. For the arts, other than architecture, there is a good select bibliography in S. C. Welch's *The Art of Mughul India*, New York, 1963. Standard works on miniature painting are Percy Brown's *Indian Painting under the Mughals*, Oxford, 1924, and I. Stchoukine's *La Peinture Indienne*, Paris, 1929, while the place of the Mughul School in the total spectrum of Indian painting is assessed in *Indian Painting* by Douglas Barrett and Basil Gray, Geneva, 1963. The visual arts patronized by the Mughul court owed much of their inspiration to Safavid influence and the Safavid achievement in architecture and painting is well illustrated in W. S. Blunt's *Isfahan, Pearl of Persia*, London, 1967. Little of value has been written on the Mughul art of gardening and C. M. Villiers Stuart's *Gardens of the Great Mughuls*, London, 1913, is merely an old-fashioned guide-book. The tradition behind the construction of these gardens, however, is discussed by V. Sackville West in an essay, 'Persian Gardens' published in *The Legacy of Persia*, edited by A. J. Arberry, Oxford, 1953, and by Donald N. Wilber in his *Persian Gardens and Garden-Pavilions*, Tokyo, 1962.

The best short guide-book to the monuments of Delhi is Y. D. Sharma's *Delhi and Its Neighbourhood*, Delhi, 1964, published by the Archaeological Survey of India which was responsible for the reports containing the detailed descriptions of the monuments of Delhi, Agra and Fatehpur Sikri. Among the older guide-books may be mentioned S. M. Latif's *Agra, Historical and Descriptive*, Calcutta, 1896; C. Stephen's *Archaeology of Delhi*, Calcutta, 1876; F. C. Fanshawe's *Delhi Past and Present*, London, 1902; G. R. Hearn's *The Seven Cities of Delhi*, London, 1906; and H. G. Keene's *Handbook for Visitors to Delhi*, Calcutta, 1906.

The rulers of Delhi up to the final establishment of the Mughul Empire by Akbar in 1556

(Only major figures in each dynasty are included)

THE SLAVE-KINGS
Qutb al-Din Aibak 1206–10
Iltutmish 1211–36
Sultana Raziyeh 1236–40
Nasir al-Din Mahmud 1246–66
Ghiyas al-Din Balban 1266–87
Muizz al-Din Kayqubad 1287–90

KHALJIS
Jalal al-Din Firuz Shah 1290–6
Ala al-Din Muhammad Shah 1296–1316
Qutb al-Din Mubarak Shah 1316–20

TUGHLUQS
Ghiyas al-Din Tughluq 1320–5
Muhammad 1325–51
Firuz Shah 1351–88

SAYYIDS
Khizr Khan 1414–21
Muhammad Shah 1434–44
Ala al-Din Alam Shah 1444–51

LODIS
Bahlul 1451–89
Iskandar 1489–1517
Ibrahim 1517–26

MUGHULS (TIMURIDS)
Babur 1526–30
Humayun 1530–40

SURS
Sher Shah 1540–5
Islam Shah 1545–54

MUGHULS (TIMURIDS)
Humayun 1555–6
Akbar 1556–1605

Genealogical table: The dynasty of the Great Mughuls

(Only those names have been included which are mentioned in the text)

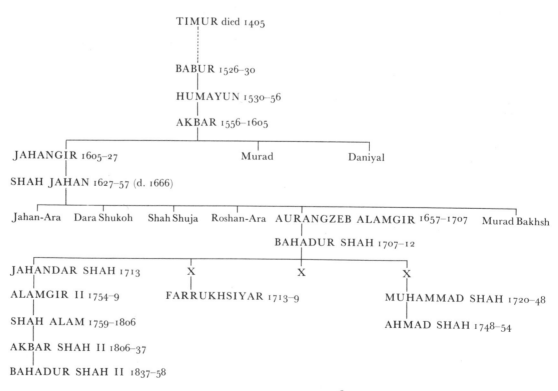

TIMUR died 1405

BABUR 1526–30

HUMAYUN 1530–56

AKBAR 1556–1605

JAHANGIR 1605–27   Murad   Daniyal

SHAH JAHAN 1627–57 (d. 1666)

Jahan-Ara   Dara Shukoh   Shah Shuja   Roshan-Ara   AURANGZEB ALAMGIR 1657–1707   Murad Bakhsh

BAHADUR SHAH 1707–12

JAHANDAR SHAH 1713   X   X   X

ALAMGIR II 1754–9   FARRUKHSIYAR 1713–9   MUHAMMAD SHAH 1720–48

SHAH ALAM 1759–1806   AHMAD SHAH 1748–54

AKBAR SHAH II 1806–37

BAHADUR SHAH II 1837–58

Index